Inside Arthur Andersen

Shifting Values,
Unexpected Consequences

Inside Arthur Andersen
Shifting Values, Unexpected Consequences

Susan E. Squires
Cynthia J. Smith
Lorna McDougall
William R. Yeack

 Prentice Hall
FINANCIAL TIMES

An Imprint of PEARSON EDUCATION
Upper Saddle River, NJ • New York • London • San Francisco • Toronto • Sydney
Tokyo • Singapore • Hong Kong • Cape Town • Madrid
Paris • Milan • Munich • Amsterdam

www.ft-ph.com

A CIP catalog record for this book can be obtained from the Library of Congress

Editorial/Production Supervisor: *MetroVoice Publishing Services*
Executive Editor: *Jim Boyd*
Editorial Assistant: *Linda Ramagnano*
Marketing Manager: *John Pierce*
Manufacturing Manager: *Alexis Heydt-Long*
Cover Design: *Anthony Gemmellaro*
Cover Design Director: *Jerry Votta*
Series Design: *Gail Cocker-Bogusz*
Full-Service Project Manager: *Anne R. Garcia*

© 2003 Pearson Education, Inc.
Publishing as Financial Times Prentice Hall
Upper Saddle River, New Jersey 07458

The publisher offers excellent discounts on this book when ordered in quantity
for bulk purchase or special sales. For more information, contact:

**U.S. Corporate and Government Sales, 1-800-382-3419, corpsales@pearsontechgroup.com.
For sales outside of the U.S., please contact: International Sales, 1-317-581-3793,
international@pearsontechgroup.com.**

Printed in the United States of America

First Printing

ISBN 0-13-140896-8

Pearson Education Ltd.
Pearson Education Australia PTY, Limited
Pearson Education Singapore, Pte. Ltd
Pearson Education North Asia Ltd
Pearson Education Canada, Ltd.
Pearson Educación de Mexico, S.A. de C.V.
Pearson Education—Japan
Pearson Education Malaysia, Pte. Ltd

FINANCIAL TIMES PRENTICE HALL BOOKS

For more information, please go to www.ft-ph.com

Business and Technology

Sarv Devaraj and Rajiv Kohli
The IT Payoff: Measuring the Business Value of Information Technology Investments

Nicholas D. Evans
Business Agility: Strategies for Gaining Competitive Advantage through Mobile Business Solutions

Nicholas D. Evans
Business Innovation and Disruptive Technology: Harnessing the Power of Breakthrough Technology…for Competitive Advantage

Nicholas D. Evans
Consumer Gadgets: 50 Ways to Have Fun and Simplify Your Life with Today's Technology…and Tomorrow's

Faisal Hoque
The Alignment Effect: How to Get Real Business Value Out of Technology

Thomas Kern, Mary Cecelia Lacity, and Leslie P. Willcocks
Netsourcing: Renting Business Applications and Services Over a Network

Ecommerce

Dale Neef
E-procurement: From Strategy to Implementation

Economics

David Dranove
What's Your Life Worth? Health Care Rationing…Who Lives? Who Dies? Who Decides?

David R. Henderson
The Joy of Freedom: An Economist's Odyssey

Jonathan Wight
Saving Adam Smith: A Tale of Wealth, Transformation, and Virtue

Entrepreneurship

Oren Fuerst and Uri Geiger
From Concept to Wall Street: A Complete Guide to Entrepreneurship and Venture Capital

David Gladstone and Laura Gladstone
Venture Capital Handbook: An Entrepreneur's Guide to Raising Venture Capital, Revised and Updated

Erica Orloff and Kathy Levinson, Ph.D.
The 60-Second Commute: A Guide to Your 24/7 Home Office Life

Jeff Saperstein and Daniel Rouach
Creating Regional Wealth in the Innovation Economy: Models, Perspectives, and Best Practices

Finance

Aswath Damodaran
The Dark Side of Valuation: Valuing Old Tech, New Tech, and New Economy Companies

Kenneth R. Ferris and Barbara S. Pécherot Petitt
Valuation: Avoiding the Winner's Curse

International Business

Peter Marber
Money Changes Everything: How Global Prosperity Is Reshaping Our Needs, Values, and Lifestyles

Fernando Robles, Françoise Simon, and Jerry Haar
Winning Strategies for the New Latin Markets

Investments

Zvi Bodie and Michael J. Clowes
Worry-Free Investing: A Safe Approach to Achieving Your Lifetime Goals

Harry Domash
Fire Your Stock Analyst! Analyzing Stocks on Your Own

Philip Jenks and Stephen Eckett, Editors
The Global-Investor Book of Investing Rules: Invaluable Advice from 150 Master Investors

Charles P. Jones
Mutual Funds: Your Money, Your Choice. Take Control Now and Build Wealth Wisely

D. Quinn Mills
Buy, Lie, and Sell High: How Investors Lost Out on Enron and the Internet Bubble

D. Quinn Mills
Wheel, Deal, and Steal: Deceptive Accounting, Deceitful CEOs, and Ineffective Reforms

John Nofsinger and Kenneth Kim
Infectious Greed: Restoring Confidence in America's Companies

John R. Nofsinger
Investment Blunders (of the Rich and Famous)…And What You Can Learn from Them

John R. Nofsinger
Investment Madness: How Psychology Affects Your Investing…And What to Do About It

Leadership

Jim Despain and Jane Bodman Converse
And Dignity for All: Unlocking Greatness through Values-Based Leadership

Marshall Goldsmith, Vijay Govindarajan, Beverly Kaye, and Albert A. Vicere
The Many Facets of Leadership

Marshall Goldsmith, Cathy Greenberg, Alastair Robertson, and Maya Hu-Chan
Global Leadership: The Next Generation

Management

Rob Austin and Lee Devin
Artful Making: What Managers Need to Know About How Artists Work

Dr. Judith M. Bardwick
Seeking the Calm in the Storm: Managing Chaos in Your Business Life

Stewart Black and Hal B. Gregersen
Leading Strategic Change: Breaking Through the Brain Barrier

William C. Byham, Audrey B. Smith, and Matthew J. Paese
Grow Your Own Leaders: How to Identify, Develop, and Retain Leadership Talent

David M. Carter and Darren Rovell
On the Ball: What You Can Learn About Business from Sports Leaders

Subir Chowdhury
Organization 21C: Someday All Organizations Will Lead this Way

Subir Chowdhury
The Talent Era: Achieving a High Return on Talent

James W. Cortada
Making the Information Society: Experience, Consequences, and Possibilities

Ross Dawson
*Living Networks: Leading Your Company, Customers, and Partners
in the Hyper-connected Economy*

Robert B. Handfield, Ph.d, and Ernest L. Nichols
Supply Chain Redesign: Transforming Supply Chains into Integrated Value Systems

Harvey A. Hornstein
*The Haves and the Have Nots: The Abuse of Power and Privilege in the Workplace...
and How to Control It*

Kevin Kennedy and Mary Moore
Going the Distance: Why Some Companies Dominate and Others Fail

Robin Miller
The Online Rules of Successful Companies: The Fool-Proof Guide to Building Profits

Fergus O'Connell
The Competitive Advantage of Common Sense: Using the Power You Already Have

Richard W. Paul and Linda Elder
Critical Thinking: Tools for Taking Charge of Your Professional and Personal Life

Matthew Serbin Pittinsky, Editor
The Wired Tower: Perspectives on the Impact of the Internet on Higher Education

W. Alan Randolph and Barry Z. Posner
*Checkered Flag Projects: 10 Rules for Creating and Managing Projects that Win,
Second Edition*

Stephen P. Robbins
The Truth About Managing People...And Nothing but the Truth

Ronald Snee and Roger Hoerl
*Leading Six Sigma: A Step-by-Step Guide Based on Experience with GE and Other
Six Sigma Companies*

Jerry Weissman
Presenting to Win: The Art of Telling Your Story

CONTENTS

ix

PREFACE

The fall of Arthur Andersen—one of the five largest accounting firms in the world—was as much a shock to its 85,000 worldwide employees as it was to the business community and the general public. Except for the Enron engagement team, those inside the global firm knew little about its association with Enron. Most first learned from the media of the Andersen felony indictment for obstructing a federal investigation. Even then, it was inconceivable to most Andersen employees that the entire firm, with offices all over the world, could be affected so profoundly. Within days, desks were being packed, families relocated, whole offices parcelled off. Everyone was left looking back at what had been. The story is poignant, not just because it affected the lives of those inside but because it has a message for businesses today in all sectors. The changes inside and outside the firm that led to actions so out of character for the company's founder, Arthur E. Andersen, are changes that can and will affect other companies, perhaps yours.

The mission of this book is to tell what happened, as seen from inside—before, during, and after—to those who are not insiders of Arthur

Andersen or the accounting industry, and provide insights for those who were insiders. The authors, Susan E. Squires, Cynthia J. Smith, Lorna McDougall, and William R. Yeack were all employed by Andersen and bring over 26 years of collective experience with the firm to the Andersen story. The book's tale is of a firm that changed as competition among the big accounting firms became aggressive. To survive and prosper, Andersen changed and adapted in ways many firms today are changing and adapting. From the days of Arthur E. Andersen's original public accounting firm that provided honest audit service, the firm became a dynamic, sprawling, more aggressive multiservice organization with clients willing to skate ever closer to the edge of risk. This book chronicles key decisions that led to changes in Andersen's culture and the external and internal factors that led to events that would have been unlikely—even impossible—only a few years before.

The story begins as Arthur Andersen goes to trial, then recounts the sequence of events that brought the firm to court—the day things turned ugly—the media coverage of the shredding, and the fall of the first of several dominos that would eventually topple Arthur Andersen.

You will get the inside view from several perspectives of the firm. What was it like to work at Arthur Andersen? How did the company grow from a small accounting firm dominated by one individual to a global firm that was the largest of its kind in the world when it became Enron's auditor? You will understand the long chain of events that eventually caused Andersen to fall. These events shed light on the role of accounting in the American economic system and on current concerns. In the end, you can consider what this means for you and perhaps for your company.

About the Authors

Arthur Andersen is a unique case to which analysis of the organizational culture can be applied. All authors are Andersen "insiders" who were participants and observers within the Andersen organization and are able to share a factual business picture, as well as a very human face of the firm's story. Three of the authors of this book are cultural experts who held positions at the firm. Based on their understanding and first-hand experience, the authors are able to shed light on events and core values of the legendary Andersen culture and how they were transformed over time, especially from 1981 to 1997, the time span of their experience.

Dr. Susan E. Squires was at Andersen Worldwide's Center of Professional Development from 1993 to 1997, working with both Arthur Andersen and Andersen Consulting as an evaluator and cultural consultant on internal and external teams.

Dr. Lorna McDougall was a cultural consultant at Andersen Worldwide, conducting research and working on long-term human resources and organizational learning for the Audit, Tax, and Consulting divisions in the U.S. and the UK.

Dr. Cynthia J. Smith, an anthropologist, began working with the firm in 1982, creating the first position for an anthropologist in the Management Development Group at Andersen's Center for Professional Education and Development in St. Charles, Illinois.

William R. Yeack's responsibilities for large multinational, high-risk projects within the firm and as a private sector executive add a front-line professional perspective to the book. William Yeack and Cynthia Smith worked closely together on cultural research projects in the firm, developing high-risk and international project cultural risk management improvements.

Acknowledgments

Many people helped us with this project. We owe thanks to the many members of the Andersen family who lent us their support, to senior members of the firm in the U.S. and UK for generously sharing their perspectives, and to all the Arthur Andersen alumni for their thoughtful interviews. We want to thank James Brennan for his generosity in terms of time and effort to help us with the interview phase of the project. All of those we talked with added immeasurably to our understanding, and without them this story might be very different.

We would like to express our deep gratitude to our editor, Jim Boyd, for the unusual opportunity to write as a team and for his invaluable insights and guidance throughout this project.

We thank Russell Hall for his editorial support and for his cheerful encouragement as we worked through the many possible approaches to writing.

We must thank Mitchell Lear for suggesting that we write this book and Dr. Leonard Sayles and Kathy Ripin for their help in thinking through the project. They gave generously of their time and advice.

We especially thank retired partner, Thad Perry, for taking an interest in the research and development projects proposed by William Yeack and Cynthia Smith when they all worked together in the early 1980s. Mr. Perry had the management courage to give permission and support for our work.

Thanks also go to Dr. Daniel Jensen, Director of the Accounting Hall of Fame at Ohio State University, who took time to engage in a most interesting and helpful discussion of recent events in accounting from his perspective as a historian of the accounting profession.

We would also like to thank those who helped us with research for the project. Elaine Lowell and Gabrielle Cooney provided help with some of the background. Brian Hickam and Tim Burns, reference librarians at Ohio State University-Mansfield Library, were extremely helpful and creative about tracking down sources.

It is important that we thank Marilyn Taillon for her Andersen insights and Kate Cox for her guidance in reorganizing the original manuscript. Bryan Bryn deserves our thanks for helping to tighten the book's conclusions.

Our families have been unfailingly supportive while we thought about and undertook the writing task. We want to express our appreciation for all the concessions our families and friends have made and for their support during our work on the book.

Lucy, Susan's dog, deserves special thanks for sitting so patiently by her desk while she wrote and rewrote instead of going for walks.

Because the firm no longer exists, for all intents and purposes, it has been difficult at times to verify information. Although we have made every effort to check points of accuracy, the authors take responsibility for any errors. When we found discrepancies in details recounted in the media, we attempted to check the facts with former Andersen partners or to decide which sources we believed to be more reliable. The story of Andersen and Enron is still unfolding, and a great deal of litigation is still outstanding against the firm, which makes it difficult for Andersen people to discuss certain topics.

1

Beginning
of the End

All-Night Shredding

David Duncan sat in the Houston courtroom and answered a question
put to him by the federal prosecutor. His face appeared strained. On
any other day, Duncan would have been in his office at Arthur Andersen, the prestigious accounting firm, or on site at Enron. He would
have been checking emails, holding a staff meeting with his audit team,
or making important calls to senior partners at Andersen's worldwide
headquarters. But on this day, he faced a judge in a federal courtroom.
His usual flamboyance had been set aside for the conservative dark suit
expected of an Andersen partner.

No one from the small Texas town of Beaumont could have dreamed
that the quiet, studious boy they had known would end up in federal
court. But Duncan had begun to change once he went away to college. At
Texas A&M, he did well in his accounting classes, joined a fraternity,

1

and learned to play golf.[1] He became competitive and ambitious. After graduation, he was recruited by the accounting giant Arthur Andersen.

Andersen was considered one of the top five accounting firms in the world. It had built its reputation on high-quality work by skilled, dedicated people. Duncan did well at Andersen and, at 35, he was elected to the Andersen partnership. Only two years later, he was asked to lead the large audit team at Enron.

At Enron, Duncan really came into his own, with the help of his close friend, Richard Causey, a former Andersen employee. The two were virtually inseparable. They worked together, went to lunch together, and played golf together. Their families even went on vacations together.[2]

Duncan took pride in his rapid rise to the top. But nothing had prepared him for his appearance in court. The courtroom remained quiet, waiting for Duncan to begin. For just an instant, David Duncan looked down at his folded hands resting on the table in front of him as though watching his career slip through his fingers. He took a breath, and people leaned forward as he began to explain his version of what had gone wrong.

"It did not particularly go well," he explained about the morning of October 23, 2001. At that time, Duncan had been the lead auditor examining the books of the Houston-based energy giant, Enron. That morning, he and several senior members of his accounting team had been invited to Enron's executive conference room to listen in on a call between several Wall Street stock analysts and Enron top executives. Enron's stock was in a downward spiral. "There were many pointed questions asked," he explained to the court. Questions were asked about Enron's audit reports and restatements.[3]

Enron was collapsing. The Securities and Exchange Commission (SEC) was starting an informal investigation. Something had to be done and quickly. Duncan called his team together in Conference Room 37C1 of the Enron building in Houston, where the Andersen audit team was located. On a good day, you can see the Gulf of Mexico from the wide plate glass windows on the 37th floor but, on that day in October, everyone was too busy to look.

Duncan told his staff they needed to start complying with Andersen's new policy on handling audit documents. The policy had been created a year and a half earlier, partly to make sure the firm's extraneous paperwork could not be used in a court case. Although the document retention policy required that paperwork supporting the firm's opinions and audit be retained, it allowed a broad category of secondary documents to be destroyed. Stunned, everybody in the room remained silent for a moment, then began racing to do what he or she had been told to do. No one asked Duncan to explain further, he testified. None of the staff asked whether what they were doing was wrong. No one questioned whether what he or she were doing might be seen as an obstruction of justice. Andersen staff just reacted, following orders without question. They were complying with a firm policy.

At Enron's offices and at Andersen's offices in Houston, Portland, Chicago, and London, the massive effort to shred files was underway. The shredders whirred steadily and noisily. The task was enormous, and both Andersen and Enron staffers worked together through the night in the days that followed. The document purge was in full swing when Andersen's own fraud investigator, David Stulb, arrived at Enron's offices in Houston. Duncan was in his office going through his email and deleting files.

"We need to get rid of this," Duncan told Stulb, pointing to his computer screen. Stulb was horrified. "Dave, you really need to keep this information," he told him. "There is a strong likelihood we will need this information." Leaving Duncan's office, Stulb made a frantic call to his boss in Andersen's New York office to let him know just how bad things were. "Dave Duncan needs some guidance on document retention," he warned.[4]

Duncan paused in his testimony, perhaps reflecting on the events he was describing. He began again. Duncan told the court that he decided to stop the shredding on November 8, after learning that the firm had received a subpoena. On that day, Duncan's assistant hurried into his office with documents marked for shredding still in her hands. This time, Duncan told his assistant, "No, you are not to shred anymore. Who's asking you to shred?" His aide stopped in her tracks, turned and headed back to her computer, where she sent an urgent email to Duncan's team. "Per Dave: no more shredding," it read. Then, she went to the office shredder, "No more shredding," she scrawled in large letters across a piece of paper and taped it to the top of the machine.[5] On November 9, the day after the SEC issued a subpoena to Andersen,[6] the shredding finally stopped.

It was too late. More than a ton of documents had already been destroyed, and over 30,000 emails and computer files, allegedly confidential to Enron, had been deleted. Evidence had been destroyed under Duncan's watch—evidence that was needed for an SEC investigation of Enron. According to Andersen's legal defense, the shredding was business as usual. The lawyers claimed that the shredding was just part of Andersen's standard practice to eliminate unnecessary files. To the SEC, it appeared to be the start of a deep cover-up operation. But, by the time Duncan appeared in court, these arguments didn't matter any more.

Duncan swayed on his feet[7] as the court told him he faced a possible jail sentence. His career was over. And with him, he would take down one of the five biggest accounting firms in the world—Arthur Andersen.

Growing Storm

There is, in Andersen, a parallel to the Titanic. Both consisted of compartmentalized units so independent that the whole was considered unsinkable. Just as the Titanic should have continued to float with some compartments flooded, Andersen employees felt the firm was designed so that the entire organization could survive, even if some of its offices were closed or if some of its partners were convicted of wrongdoing. That one office of the firm could sink the firm was unthinkable.

After all, Andersen was one of the Big Five—the top five accounting firms in the world—along with Deloitte Touche Tohmatsu, KPMG, PricewaterhouseCoopers, and Ernst & Young. By 2002, a reputation for quality services had helped Andersen grow to almost 350 offices in major cities throughout 84 countries, with 85,000 worldwide employees serving 100,000 clients, including governments and multinational corporations. Along with traditional accounting and auditing services, and tax advice, Andersen had evolved into a multidisciplinary professional services partnership offering a range of business consulting and information technology services.

Andersen had more than once been number one among the giants in the accounting industry. In the 1980s, the eight firms dominating the accounting profession were jokingly referred to as "Arthur Andersen and the Seven Dwarfs." Andersen was number one among the Big Five until its split with Andersen Consulting sent Arthur Andersen into fifth place. In 2000, Andersen Consulting became an independent public corporation known as Accenture. But Arthur Andersen seemed unsinkable and was rebounding after Andersen Consulting broke loose from the parent firm. How could one of its local office compartments sink such a ship of commerce?

Enron

To understand why Arthur Andersen was brought down, you first have to understand what Enron did wrong. Until it was brought to the public's attention for its mishandling of funds, Enron was not a household name, nor was Arthur Andersen. Not many utilities ever reach that level of public visibility. Within energy circles, however, it was well known as one of the few companies to successfully integrate energy exploration, transmission, and selling. At its peak, Enron's service companies included Florida Gas Transmission, Midwestern Gas Transmission, New Power Company, Northern Border Pipeline, Portland

General Electric, Transwestern Pipe, and Enron South America, in addition to Enron Energy Services, Enron Wholesale, and EnronOnline, among others.[8]

Enron had been created in 1985 by the merger of two gas pipeline companies: Houston Natural Gas and InterNorth. Ken Lay, a native of rural Missouri, was CEO of Houston Natural Gas. From his early beginnings as the son of a small-time farmer, Lay had managed to work his way through school to earn a Ph.D. in economics. Although Lay was never a strong manager, according to the people who worked for him,[9] he had developed into a clever strategist. He quickly saw the potential in gas deregulation and engineered the merger. Enron became an important lobbyist for energy deregulation.

In 1985, the same year that Enron was created, the U.S. federal government issued new regulations that supported a market pricing system in the natural gas industry, based on supply and demand. This meant that the price of natural gas would depend on how many people wanted to buy it. If supply was low and lots of people wanted natural gas, the price would go up. If supply was high or no one wanted to buy, the price would drop.

Under deregulation, prices began to fluctuate. Buyers and sellers of energy realized that they could no longer predict the price of natural gas. Once again, Ken Lay saw opportunity in this fluctuation and, with the advice of Enron executive Jeffrey Skilling, a Harvard MBA, Enron became a broker for trading energy.[10]

Enron offered buyers and sellers an innovative strategy for pricing stability through long-term contracts in which the value of energy in the contract was calculated using formulas that extended the current market price and market predictions into the future. This seemed fair. But everyone soon found out that setting a market value for energy to be purchased as far as ten or more years in the future is not easy. Enron's customer contracts were difficult to value because no one could truly predict future market value of the energy that was being bought and sold in the contracts. Enron had to produce figures for its accountants and ultimately for its stockholders to show that the company was making a profit.

To predict the future price of the energy in these long-term contracts, Enron used computer models designed to forecast energy needs and prices. The computer models predicted strong demand for energy in the future. Strong demand meant that the future market value of the energy in the long-term contracts Enron held would be high. This suggested high future profits for Enron. In the late 1980s and early 1990s, Enron found that it was making money buying and selling the natural gas contracts themselves. Next, Ken Lay and Jeffrey Skilling decided to try their hands at electricity. Enron began to corner the electricity market by buying up electricity-generation facilities and securing long-term electricity contracts similar to those it had negotiated for gas. Again, this was a great success and a big money-maker for Enron, which was becoming a very powerful utility company.

By the mid 1990s, Enron had a commanding place in the energy industry as one of the largest energy dealers in the United States. The company's success in gas and electricity encouraged it to branch out even more. Enron used the profits from its successful energy businesses to get into other commodity markets, such as paper and chemicals, where it had less expertise. The company also began to speculate in the high-risk high-tech sector, at that time a favorite of stockbrokers and a money-maker. In 1998 alone, Enron's stock had risen an extraordinary 89 percent. In 1999, it gained another 58 percent.

Enron's belief in itself, its misleading accounting practices, and its strong connections to Wall Street firms sustained Enron's stock until the very end. Even as evidence of fraud was amassing and the stock price was plummeting, stock analysts were recommending the company's stock to investors. If any analyst or auditor challenged their methods, Enron executives would explain that there was nothing wrong with their "new economy" models. In fact, the Enron executives could be downright rude to anyone who challenged the wisdom of their models, suggesting that those questioning might not have the brainpower to understand. But those models were flawed, and Enron's arrogance was a cover-up for inconsistencies in Enron's financial situation.

Enron's success story began to unravel in April 2001 when it made public its first-quarter earnings for that year. While the company reported an 18 percent increase in revenue, the detailed accounting behind this number did not support the earnings claim. Instead of profits, the numbers suggested that the company might actually be losing money. Enron's stock slid from $80 a share to $60 as the news of its potential losses was released to the public. It continued to slide when, on October 16, 2001, Enron took a one-time charge of just over $1 billion and admitted to losses of $618 million.[11] To ease the fears of stockholders, Enron executives explained that the charges would be one-time and nonrecurring. This explanation was more a hope than a guarantee. Concerned that describing the charges as nonrecurring was misleading, Andersen's auditors advised Enron's managers against this characterization.[12]

Andersen's auditors were right. Less than one month later, on November 8, 2001, Enron restated financial reports for 1997, 1998, 1999, 2000, and the first three quarters of 2001. Altogether, Enron added $2.59 billion of debt to its books and wiped out about 20 percent of its earnings for the previous five years. By the end of November 2001, Enron's stock had fallen so low that it was considered worthless. Enron declared bankruptcy in December 2001.

Enron had been able to obscure its losses by manipulating its financial relationships with numerous partner companies, called *Special-Purpose Entities* (SPEs). It is not illegal or even unusual to set up such "off-the-books" partnerships to improve the bottom line, raise cash, or manage debts. The profits or losses of an SPE do not have to show up on the books of a parent company if the SPE is independently owned. To be classified as a legitimate SPE for Enron, the company had to meet three criteria:

1. At least 3 percent of the SPE's stock could not be held by Enron,

2. Enron could not control the SPE, and

3. Enron was not responsible for any loans or losses of the SPE.

Enron created as many as 3,500 SPEs[13] with names such as Chewco, Raptor, JEDI, and Merlin. Later, SEC investigations determined that some of the SPEs did not qualify as independent partners. For example, Michael Kopper, an Enron employee, headed Chewco. The case should have been made that Enron controlled Chewco because one of Enron's employees ran the company. It wasn't. In another case, it turned out that Enron owned all but 1.5 percent of JEDI stock. JEDI debt should have shown up on Enron's accounting books. It didn't.

Some Enron employees were starting to get worried. Margaret Ceconi, a one-time Enron Energy Services employee, became suspicious of the way Enron was manipulating some of the SPEs. Although she had an accounting degree, she was not an accountant at Enron. To validate her suspicions without causing a stir, she wrote to the SEC, using her personal email account. In her email, she laid out a simple hypothetical example, describing what she had observed. "Say you have a food company that makes both hot dogs and ice cream. The hot dog stand is making money, and the ice cream stand is losing money. So the company puts the ice cream losses on the profitable hot dog books." Then she asked, "Since both the ice cream stand and the hot dog stand have the same owner, is this legal?" A member of the SEC replied to the email that the practices described in Ceconi's example misrepresented the performance of each of the food stands. However, they would have to know the exact circumstances to determine illegal activity with certainty.[14]

Using accounting practices similar to those described in the hot dog and ice cream stand switch, Enron hid its losses and boosted its earning figures. One of the four Raptor SPEs, hid Enron debt of over $1 billion alone. To avoid showing debt, Enron used a second trick.

The company manipulated the computer-generated values assigned to the energy contracts it held to show greater potential earnings than the company really had. Enron then sold these contracts to investment bankers. In return, Enron agreed to buy back the energy in the contracts. In effect, these clever deals amounted to disguised loans. It looked like Enron had made a profitable sale. Instead, it had really borrowed money based on the value of the contract with a promise to pay it back—a loan. None of this was reported accurately in Enron's quarterly reports. By the time Enron's deceptive practices were revealed, investors with funds in Enron lost an estimated $60 billion.

The sheer size of the case is overwhelming. How could a company like Enron hide its true level of debt unnoticed by the Andersen auditors who had been overseeing Enron's books since its creation in 1985?

Arthur Andersen

Enron was a very important client for Arthur Andersen. It was as Enron's auditor, Arthur Andersen found itself at the center of one of the biggest bankruptcies in U.S. history.

For 89 years, Arthur Andersen was a mainstay of the accounting profession holding a reputation for honesty and trustworthiness. Over time, Arthur Andersen had also developed a reputation for experience and reliability in the utility industries, and some of the first Andersen clients had been Midwestern utilities. Andersen had specialized in handling companies such as Enron. The firm had been InterNorth's auditor and continued to be retained by Enron after the merger of InterNorth and Houston Natural Gas in 1985. Andersen was the logical choice to conduct Enron's federally required independent audit.

By March 2002, facing a felony charge for obstructing a federal investigation of Enron, Andersen's reputation was lost. Once the firm was indicted, Andersen rapidly lost its audit clients. The core of its business was in ruins.[15] On Saturday, August 31, 2002, Arthur Andersen ceased to be an auditing firm of publicly traded companies.

With its strong background in auditing utilities and its long history with InterNorth and Enron, Andersen auditors should have uncovered wrongdoing at Enron as soon as it occurred. Perhaps.

A review of the accountant's job may help to clarify why the Andersen auditors did not report Enron's questionable dealings and losses earlier. Typically, companies employ their own accountants to handle their financial reporting. External auditors are independent accountants hired by the company's board of directors, usually with input from the chief financial officer or management team, to check the work of the company's internal financial managers and accountants. Federal regulations implemented in 1933 and 1934 require all U.S. publicly traded corporations to have an external audit once a year to protect the people who own the company from mismanagement of funds and fraud. The federal government felt the regulation was necessary because the speculative investment in publicly traded companies during America's Roaring Twenties had encouraged managers and owners to inflate stock prices. The 1929 market crash had triggered a decade-long economic depression. The external auditors are hired to verify that the internal accountants have done their work accurately.

Everyone who owns stock in a company or that has a retirement plan or mutual fund that is invested in stock is an owner and receives an annual financial report based, in part, on an audit of internal records by independent accountants. These audited reports are generally long, complicated appendices to the annual reports. The auditors must come to an opinion about whether the financial statements made by the company are accurate and based on Generally Accepted Accounting Practices (GAAP) and Generally Accepted Accounting Standards (GAAS). The audit reports often appear with qualifying statements containing information critical to assessing a company's financial condition. Although not required to be auditor-certified, companies also file quarterly reports with the SEC.

It is important to bear in mind that most auditors are not trained in criminal investigation. They don't conduct audits as though they are on a crime scene. Most of the time, their work is pretty routine. Auditors look at accounts receivable and at expenditures. They check to see whether the methods for recording transactions are appropriate and consistent. But they don't look at everything. They certainly don't spend much time looking for evidence against the very people who hired them. They don't bug people's phones. They don't hide in the corporate basement until nightfall, then sneak upstairs to look for hidden files. They can't. Even with the help of computers, the typical large company has so many transactions that a team of auditors cannot cover all of them in detail. Instead, they may take a sampling of transactions or check the accounting processes and the information technology (IT) systems. If the sample is okay and the systems appear sound, most auditors will conclude that the company's financial accounting is fine. As one former employee of Andersen explained, auditors look at financial systems maintained by the company and see whether the system is secure.

Even though an auditor might conclude that a company's financial system and reports seem appropriate and accurate, there is plenty of flexibility for differences of opinion. Accountants often have several options about how they calculate and report corporate finances. Indeed, the more complex corporate finances become, the more options will present themselves. The Financial Accounting Standards Board (FASB) guidelines that provide generally accepted accounting standards contain over 100,000 pages of rules. Matching a potential problem with the applicable rule can be a lengthy and interpretive process. Although the guidelines are cumbersome to use, the big accounting firms, including Andersen, lobbied to keep the status quo. They fought tough new reforms because their audit clients liked the flexibility.

The Andersen auditors looking at Enron's books did find irregularities in how Enron reported or did not report losses. In particular, they were concerned about Enron's SPEs. By 1999, Andersen auditors clearly stated to Enron's board of directors that Enron's manipulation of funds through its SPEs was suspect. David Duncan himself warned the Enron board of directors that, "...many [of the SPEs] push limits and have a high risk profile." But Duncan did not indicate that he thought this was a big concern.[16] The SPEs were high risk, but were they illegal? That was up to interpretation, based on the facts the auditors had at the time. Later, in court, Duncan claimed that none of the Andersen auditors had all the information to interpret accurately whether rules had been broken.[17]

Although it may have been true that Andersen auditors did not have all the information concerning the full extent of Enron's transactions, Duncan could not say that he was entirely unaware. Andersen's Professional Standards Group (PSG) had advised against going along with some of Enron's deals. As far back as May 1999, Benjamin Neuhausen, a member of the PSG, wrote Duncan, saying, "Setting aside the accounting, [the] idea of a venture entity managed by [Enron's] CFO is terrible from a business point of view [with] conflicts of interest galore. Why would any director in his or her right mind ever approve such a scheme?" Numerous memos objecting to Enron transactions were also written by Carl Bass, another member of the PSG.[18]

On February 5, 2001, just before Enron's business practices were questioned publicly in April, 13 Andersen partners held a routine annual risk assessment meeting to decide whether to retain Enron as a client. The discussion raised issues about possible conflicts of interest associated with Enron's SPEs. Duncan gave his fellow partners reassuring explanations. Despite ongoing warnings from the PSG, the partners were reassured and the decision was made to stick with Enron. Later, Michael Jones, one of the Andersen partners who attended the meeting, wrote, "It appeared that we [Andersen] had the appropriate people and processes in place to serve Enron and manage our engagement risks."[19] The Andersen partners put their confidence in David Duncan and the auditors on his team.

Given the arrogant and aggressive nature of Enron's corporate culture, one must wonder whether the Andersen team was equipped to stand up to Enron executives. A warning of possible wrongdoing from Arthur Andersen traditionally carried enough weight to convince a reluctant client. It was in the client's own interest. But Enron's leaders thought they knew better. They were also prepared to "strong-arm" Andersen's hapless auditors to get their way. In one account, Enron managers were said to have cornered an Andersen auditor in a small conference room where they demanded an opinion letter that would support a claim for $270 million in tax credits. When the Andersen auditor resisted being rushed to deliver an opinion, one of the Enron managers shoved a chair under the doorknob while another explained, "Nobody leaves until I get that opinion letter." After 30 minutes of badgering by the Enron managers, the Andersen auditor agreed to provide the opinion that afternoon in exchange for his release.[20]

While Andersen's senior partners might have withstood any client's intimidation tactics, Andersen's younger and more inexperienced auditors were definitely not yet strong enough to stand alone. Some partners privately worried that Duncan was too young and inexperienced to handle such an aggressive client. Although the once-quiet Duncan had developed a self-confident Texas bravado at Enron, it seemed to be more of a show than real change.

Even Enron employees, including Sherron Watkins, an ex-Andersen accountant who suspected trouble, had to proceed cautiously. Watkins had worked for Enron for eight years. By the late 1990s, she was assigned to work on some of the SPEs' off-the-books deals. When she realized what was happening, she sent an anonymous, one-page letter to Enron's CEO, Ken Lay, about what she had observed while working with one of the four Raptor SPEs. She pointed out the "funny accounting" and warned, "I am incredibly nervous that we [Enron] will implode in a wave of accounting scandals."[21]

Her fears were well founded. In a painful twist of fate, it was the later publication of Watkins' own memo that convicted Enron and Andersen in the court of public opinion, if not the federal courts.

Everybody was still in shock from the tragic events of September 11th. Private and institutional investors were losing billions. Pensions were being eroded and, in some cases, wiped out. Americans everywhere had also watched as the Western states fought against energy companies that were manipulating energy supplies and imposing exorbitant prices on their customers to generate quick cash. Meanwhile, SEC investigators were uncovering a host of self-serving alliances between brokers, bankers, lawyers, venture capitalists, analysts, and corporate executives. It became easier to think that most of the money these people made came from a coordinated effort to push a company into the public market, grab stock, and cash in by selling their own stock to unsuspecting public investors just before the stock crashed. People wondered what other corporations had misleading—or just plain incorrect—financial reports. Together, Enron and Andersen became examples of seemingly pervasive corporate collusion that made Americans doubt the companies they invested in. Enron's financial scandal was depressing the stock market. Enron employees and all the other folks who had invested in Enron stock were feeling the effects.

The SEC had already opened an informal investigation based on the October 16 financial report, and by October 31, 2001, the SEC had upgraded its investigation from informal to formal. Now, with the November 8 restatement, they became more dubious. The SEC suspicions concentrated on Enron's complex financial partnerships—the SPEs—and the appropriateness of practices Enron used to keep certain transactions off the books and out of sight. Investigators were searching for accounting rules that had been broken.

The press began to build up the drama in the months before the Andersen trial actually began in May of 2002. In January 2002, the *Wall Street Journal* declared "the scandal is not quite here yet but the elements are all there."[22] An ABC television news program reported that Enron and Andersen staff had kept shredding documents even after a company directive was issued to stop. The *Wall Street Journal* painted a vivid picture of shredding, describing a conveyor belt whisking "confidential files of major law and consulting firms, investment banks, and other businesses into rows of gnashing blades, which slice them into tangled ribbons…then get recycled into toilet tissue."[23]

After Enron's bankruptcy proceedings began, evidence of the extent and nature of Enron's financial transgressions began to mount. On January 23, 2002, Kenneth Lay, Enron's CEO, resigned as chairman and chief executive of Enron. By January 31, 2002, both the SEC and the House Committee on Energy and Commerce were asking questions about Enron's many complex partnership deals. Media attention now turned from Andersen to its client, Enron. The idea of a shredding machine churning paper into pulp had been an image that the media could dramatize. Now it was old news.

Andersen on Trial

Andersen's guilt may have seemed clear to the public but jurors hearing the federal court proceedings had a much more difficult time coming to a judgment.

On May 13, 2002, David Duncan, the lead Andersen auditor on the Enron account, confessed to ordering the shredding of Enron files. In so doing, "I obstructed justice," he admitted.[24] Even though David Duncan finally admitted to obstruction of justice, the shredding, which attracted so much media attention, turned out to be unimportant. Important documents had not been shredded or were reconstructed with Andersen's help. The evidence was too flimsy for the jury to determine whether there had been criminal intent. The business of the shredding was "superficial and largely circumstantial, and it had a lot to do with Andersen just tidying up their files," Oscar Criner, foreman of the jury, related after the event.[25]

Also in Andersen and Duncan's favor was the fact that, by November 8, 2001, Andersen's auditors had helped revise Enron statements for the previous five years to reflect reductions in previously reported net income and report debt accurately. The restatement reduced the earnings for that period and put $2.59 billion of debt on Enron's books. Corporations do not like restatements of earnings, which tend to disclose unpleasant financial realities. Although Andersen did advise Enron to make the restatement, it was not a popular move for Andersen or for Enron. It made them both look incompetent at best. The earnings restatements revealed serious financial shortfalls. By December 2, 2001, Enron had filed for bankruptcy.

It was clear that Andersen had failed to keep Enron on track. But it was still not clear that Andersen had committed the obstruction of justice felony. In its public defense, Andersen executives told the Senate Permanent Subcommittee on Investigations that Enron had withheld crucial data about its finances. Eventually, the Department of Justice was left with little against Andersen. It finally indicted the firm on one charge of obstruction of justice because the company had allegedly withheld, altered, and destroyed evidence the SEC needed to investigate Enron. Andersen's trial began on May 17, 2002 and ran until June 16.

Before sending the jury to deliberate, the trial judge, Melinda Harmon, gave the jury a particularly long and detailed set of instructions about how to carry out its duties. She warned them that the evidence provided by David Duncan, who had agreed to testify for the prosecution in exchange for leniency in his sentencing, was to be treated with special care. The jury soon recognized that they would not be able to agree on whether Duncan was telling the whole truth. When the jury started its deliberations on June 5, they were divided 50–50. "Some of us believed him and some of us didn't," foreman Oscar Criner said afterward. Whatever the truth, it was clear that Duncan had a lot of baggage. On June 8, the jury was still split 9–3 but now more of the jurors were in favor of conviction.[26]

By June 12, the jury was still deadlocked, and it looked as though a mistrial would have to be declared. Judge Harmon told the jury to go back and try once again to reach a unanimous verdict. The jurors had taken hundreds of pages of notes, and they consulted them again. They could not come to a unanimous decision about *who* the wrongdoer was. They asked the judge whether they could come to a verdict if they were convinced that wrong had been done but were not sure by whom.

Judge Harmon ruled that they could. The incriminating evidence that the jurors finally settled on came from a memo written by an Andersen in-house attorney based in Chicago and not from Duncan's confession. At the trial, Andersen lawyers argued that key records associated with the Enron audit had been carefully maintained and not shredded, as alleged by the prosecution. Andersen then produced these documents to demonstrate its claim and assisted in reconstructing the documents that had been shredded and deleted. Not everything had been shredded. Duncan *had* kept detailed records about Enron's audits, including memos about his own handling of sensitive issues, such as Enron's need to restate third-quarter earnings for the previous year.

The audit records documented that Enron had accumulated $618 million in losses by 2000 and needed to take just over $1 billion in write-offs. Enron wanted these write-offs to be characterized as "nonrecurring" and wanted Andersen to back it up. As a one-time event, the information could be portrayed to stockholders as an unusual occurrence. It would never happen again, Enron could assure everyone. A memo written by Duncan clearly showed that he had disagreed with Enron and thought these statements were inaccurate. Taking a new direction in the prosecution, the federal attorneys had introduced an email written by Andersen attorney, Nancy Temple. Temple, who had worked for the firm only 18 months, had suggested that Duncan's memo be altered to change the word *misleading* in a description of Enron's accounting practices, as the memo originally stated. Temple asked for the change after the fact to make it appear that Andersen had not failed to report its objections to the "nonrecurring" characterization, which an auditor had a duty to do. Also, Temple requested that her name be removed from the email.[27] To the jury, this looked like a cover-up. It was in this email that the jury found evidence of intentional corruption. They convicted the firm on this single memo from Andersen's in-house attorney, Nancy Temple, to David Duncan and not because of shredded documents or deleted emails.

Andersen employees worldwide were stunned. The indictment itself had already condemned Andersen, even though employees felt that the damages should be limited to the Houston office and David Duncan. According to common understandings of the basic partnership agreement, the Houston office employees were empowered to make their own decisions and run the office the way they saw fit, as long as the office maintained professional accounting standards and followed Andersen's quality assurance processes. Each partner was expected to abide by the terms of the partnership agreement and decisions that the entire partnership made. David Duncan and the Houston office had shown poor judgment, making questionable decisions that did not accurately reflect the firm or the position it took on some of Enron's transactions. Even if an Andersen partner was found guilty of wrong-doing, the entire firm should not be branded as criminal.

As far away as the city of Taipei in Taiwan, Andersen protesters carried "scapegoat" placards in the streets. In Washington, DC, freshly scrubbed junior staff members embarking on their audit careers marched, wearing their sweatshirts with the Andersen logo. They were hurt and angered, too. Despite the conviction, they did not feel guilty of any crime, even by association, and they wanted people to know it.

The protesters were not ready to accept liability. Andersen was a limited liability partnership (LLP) and could be indicted and convicted in its entirety. Andersen had used the LLP organizational type to legally avoid unlimited individual liability that general partnerships faced. Although the LLP organization limits the personal financial liability for members of the partnership, the partnership could still bear civil and criminal liability. In Andersen's case, if the Houston office was guilty, all offices across America could be found guilty, too. The inherent legal consequence of the partnership structure and the effect of the obstruc-tion-of-justice conviction on those who had no direct connection with the crime made it hard for anyone associated with the Andersen name. Everyone in the company would share the burden of guilt.

With Andersen's conviction, the public was satisfied that justice had been served. It took longer for the deeper consequences to be felt. The disgrace of Arthur Andersen and Enron affected large and small investors alike. Confidence in audit reports was lost. People began pulling out of the stock market, already shaky after the failure of so many dot-com companies. The markets slumped further. And, in the wake of Enron and the Andersen conviction, many corporations found a need to restate their earnings. They correctly feared further withdrawal of investments if they did not. The Justice Department began a series of indictments against analysts, CEOs, CFOs, and other officers of companies.

There were other substantial effects, most of which are still developing. The head of the SEC, Harvey Pitt, resigned. He had been criticized because his own associations with accounting firms, legal firms, and brokerages might suggest conflicts of interest. When he suggested a choice for the head of a new public oversight body whose ethics turned out to be seriously flawed, it was the last straw, and he stepped down.

The federal government and accounting associations initiated their own reviews of accounting practices and standards. The CEOs and CFOs of nearly 200 companies that were registered in the U.S. were forced by the SEC to assume personal liability for the accuracy of their company's reports. Government regulators, the media, and professional investors alike began taking a close look at the seemingly pervasive conflicts of interest between corporate managers, boards, auditors, investment bankers, stock analysts, brokers, and lawyers.

In Search of an Explanation: Culture of Greed or Culture Change

Most people prefer quick and easy answers whenever corporate scandals occur. Arguments focusing on a "culture of greed" or "poor management," "difficult clients," "immorality," and "governmental incompetence" are all convenient abstractions that tell us that the people or institutions involved were corrupt or incompetent. The media blamed the "culture of greed" for the bad corporate behavior at Enron and at Andersen. But what does that really mean?

During the entire investigation and trial, no one even suggested that Andersen employees were involved in personal gain. Duncan was reported to be making between $600,000 and $1 million a year. In contrast, his friend Richard Causey, Enron's Chief Accounting Officer, cashed in over $13 million in stock options between 1998 and 2001. Enron stock options and bonuses did not end up in the pockets of Andersen employees.

Although the desire to be rich is a powerful motivator, it obscures far more important lessons that could help Americans avoid catastrophic business failures in the future. And, of course, Andersen auditors had resisted the temptation of personal gain in hundreds of thousands of cases over its nine decades in business. The SEC, the accounting profession, and the giant accounting firms, including Andersen, were built on the assumption that businesses are accountable to stockholders and the public at large, should abide by the laws of the land, and should be independently monitored. No one knew better than Andersen employees that accounting professionals are often exposed to what one partner referred to as "skullduggery."[28] It's always been the auditor's job to make sure that this does not affect investors.

Although more complex explanations or explanations with more than one cause can be difficult to understand, the deepest insights often come from explanations that recognize several factors. Greed could certainly have been a factor in Andersen's decision to continue auditing Enron—clearly a challenging client. As one of Andersen's biggest clients, Enron paid them over $52 million in fees in 2000, and fees were expected to shoot up to $100 million soon. Was it the fees that motivated Duncan and the partnership to keep Enron as a client, even though it was considered high risk? A senior member of the firm noted sadly that Andersen would have walked away from such a risky client 10 years earlier. What changed in the firm's culture and in the U.S.

business environment that encouraged Andersen partners to compromise their founding values?

There is more to the explanation than simply greed. As you go through the pages that follow in this book, you will have an opportunity to form your own conclusions about the end of Andersen. Is the story a tragedy about a great many people who were hurt by a few bad apples? Or, as some believe, is the heart of the story about the government doing the wrong thing in going after Andersen, the firm, instead of limiting its attack to specific individuals in the company?

We hope you will find that the theme is not simply a picture of greed that overwhelmed corporate values. Rather, the real story is about a firm that changed in a way that inadvertently created the seeds of its own destruction. This is a multigenerational saga that will take you from the early years of the firm to its final days. From Arthur E. Andersen's original partnership, a new firm evolved that became a dynamic, sprawling, more aggressive giant, with clients willing to skate ever closer to the edge of acceptable business and legal risk.

You will see that each generation of Andersen employees was faced with crucial choices about Andersen's direction. In the beginning, Andersen became successful because it followed clear guidelines and molded first-rate accountants. However, following the death of Arthur Andersen, the firm grew far larger than Arthur Andersen thought was wise by increasingly offering clients consulting services in addition to audit. Together, growth and drift from core services challenged accountability and leadership. The decisions the firm's leaders made at each point sent the firm down an ever more tangled path and, ultimately, to the firm's collapse. You will explore the stages of change that led to an evolved complex structure, and you will consider the external and internal factors that led to the changes. Most important of all, you may find that those factors and changes are not too different from those affecting companies all across the country and the world.

The firm ceased auditing publicly traded companies on August 31, 2001. "They killed us," an Andersen partner told reporters after the trial, "for no good reason."[29]

These are only the bare facts of an American business tragedy. What follows will let you share in the in-depth details of what led to the unraveling of one of the five biggest accounting firms in the world.

References

1. McRoberts, Flynn. 2002. "Ties to Enron Blinded Andersen." *Chicago Tribune*, September 3.

2. Bryce, Robert. 2002. *Pipe Dreams: Greed, Ego, and the Death of Enron*. New York: Public Affairs. p. 238.

3. Johnson, Carrie. 2002. "Star Witness Offers More Damaging Testimony about Andersen." *Washington Post*. May 14.

4. McRoberts, Flynn 2002. "Greed Tarnished Golden Reputation." *Chicago Tribune*, September 1.

5. McRoberts, Flynn. 2002. "Ties to Enron Blinded Andersen." *Chicago Tribune*, September 3.

6. Timeline of Events Surrounding Andersen Document Destruction. 2002. *www.findlaw.com*. Accessed November 23, 2002.

7. McRoberts, Flynn. 2002. "Ties to Enron Blinded Andersen." *Chicago Tribune*, September 3.

8. Hale, Briony. 2002. Enron's Internet Monster. *http://news.bbc.co.uk/1/low/business/1684503.stm* Accessed December 14.

9. Bryce, Robert. 2002. *Pipe Dreams: Greed, Ego, and the Death of Enron*. New York: Public Affairs. p. 30.

10. Fox, Loren. 2002. *Enron: The Rise and Fall*. New York: John Wiley & Sons. p. 34.

11. Fox, Loren. 2002. *Enron: The Rise and Fall*. New York: John Wiley & Sons.

12. Garza, Melita Marie. 2002. "Altered Memo Key to Verdict," *Chicago Tribune*, June 16.

13. Summary of the corporate scandal sheet compiled by the Nader organization.

14. McRoberts, Flynn. 2002. "Ties to Enron Blinded Andersen," *Chicago Tribune*, September 3.

15. Glater, Jonathan D. 2002. "Andersen's Partners are Vital Part of Rescue Proposal," *New York Times*. March 26.

16. Fox, Loren. 2002. *Enron: The Rise and Fall*. New York: John Wiley & Sons. p. 158.

17. AAA Flash: USA: Trail of Complaints about Andersen. 1/28/2002. *http://support .casals.com/aaaflash1/busca.asp?ID_AAAControl=6615.* Accessed December 12, 2002.

18. McRoberts, Flynn, 2002. "Ties to Enron Blinded Andersen," *Chicago Tribune.* September 3.

19. Fox, Loren. 2002. *Enron: The Rise and Fall.* New York: John Wiley & Sons. p. 229.

20. Bryce, Robert. 2002. *Pipe Dreams: Greed, Ego, and the Death of Enron.* Public Affairs: New York. p. 232–233

21. McRoberts, Flynn, 2002. "Repeat Offender Gets Stiff Justice," *Chicago Tribune,* September 4.

22. *Wall Street Journal.* 2002. January.

23. "Duncan Admits Guilt in Enron Shredding," *Houston Chronicle,* May 13, 2002.

24. Johnson, Carrie. 2002. "Enron Auditor Admits Crime." *Washington Post,* May 14.

25. McRoberts, Flynn. 2002. "Ties to Enron Blinded Andersen," *Chicago Tribune,* September 3.

26. Garza, Melita Marie. 2002. "Altered Memo Key to Verdict," *Chicago Tribune,* June 16.

27. Ivanovich, David and Mary Flood. 2002. "Andersen Faces Fire in Court this Week," *Houston Chronicle,* May 6.

28. Glickauf, Joseph. 1971. "Foot Steps Towards Professionalism," In *Footsteps Towards Professionalism: The Development of an Administrative Services Practice over the Past Twenty-Five Years,* Chicago: Arthur Andersen & Co. p. 95.

29. McRoberts, Flynn. 2002. "Ties to Enron Blinded Andersen," *Chicago Tribune,* September 3.

2

HONEST BEGINNINGS

On November 8, 2001, the day the SEC issued a subpoena to Arthur Andersen, it was business as usual at the firm. The firm had built a reputation for being tough and honest as it expanded into a network of approximately 350 freestanding local offices in 84 countries throughout the world. Andersen's 85,000 employees were aware of Enron's troubles but few anticipated the extent or severity of the outcome. Andersen had weathered rough storms in the past, and most staff assumed this one would pass, too. Andersen's staff shared a common understanding that the acts of one office or one individual were not a reflection of the entire firm.

As one of the top accounting firms in the world, Arthur Andersen had gained a reputation as a tough, competent, and honest firm. It earned its world-class status and influence over the course of its 89-year history. Large clients paid millions in fees to have Andersen audit their financial statements. An Andersen partner could stride into an executive office or boardroom in any of the world's major companies with confidence. Their clients listened when Andersen partners or staff talked. Andersen auditors had the authority to approve or question the books of publicly held companies, and a negative Andersen opinion might trigger scrutiny from the SEC.

To understand the extent to which Arthur Andersen changed over its 89-year history, you can benefit from a look back to the firm's beginning. As you become acquainted with the blunt, candid man who founded the firm and gave it his name, the differences in the firm at the time of its demise will be all the more striking. Many attributed the establishment of Andersen's reputation directly to Arthur E. Andersen, the firm's founder. His life story is the embodiment of the American belief in an individual's ability to succeed through strong values and hard work. The extent to which his experiences and principles were exemplified in his firm 50 years after his death is a study in how to expand a professional firm.

Founding Father, Founding Values

Arthur Andersen, the fourth of eight children, was born in 1885 in Plano, a small, rural Illinois town, to John and Mary Andersen. His parents were Norwegian immigrants who came to the U.S. in 1882. Arthur's father eventually found a job as a foundry foreman at Fraser & Chalmers.

His family's dreams of a better life came to an end with the early death of both parents. Arthur was an orphan by the age of 16. The children were separated, and Arthur's four younger siblings went to live with relatives. Arthur and his three older brothers were left on their own, and Arthur needed a job. One of his father's employers, William Chalmers, took Arthur under his wing. He gave Arthur a job in the mail room and helped him out financially so he could finish his education at night. Arthur never forgot the support he received from his patron, and throughout his life, he tried to help other bright, working-class young men who needed a hand up. He was known to particularly favor those who had overcome adversity by hard work.[1]

Arthur E. Andersen's early experiences shaped his personality. He did not develop trust easily. His contemporaries described him as a stern, demanding man who set himself high standards for hard work and long hours that would later be expected from the accountants who worked for him. While working at Fraser & Chalmers during the day, he attended high school, then took college courses at night. After graduation, he taught at Northwestern University's new School of Commerce. At the same time, he was working his way up from mail-room clerk to assistant controller of the company.

Although he worked long hours at his job and was studying for his certified public accountant (CPA) exam, he made time in his life to court Emma Barnes Arnold. He married her in 1906, when he was just 21 years old. They had two daughters, Ethyl and Dorothy, and one son, Arthur Arnold. It is not clear how much time he actually had for his family during the early years. "He was a stern, no-nonsense man who focused entirely on business and did not mix easily with others—not even his partners," one of Arthur's partners, Leonard Spacek, would later reminisce.[2]

In 1907, he left Fraser & Chalmers to join Price Waterhouse & Co. His wife, Emma, was horrified to learn he had taken a significant pay cut to join the accounting firm. She worried that Arthur was putting his ambition ahead of his new family's security.[3] A year later, in 1908, he became Illinois' youngest CPA at the age of 23. He was well on his way to a successful accounting career. After three years with Price Waterhouse, he left to become controller for Schlitz, the Milwaukee, Wisconsin brewing company. While working for Schlitz, he commuted 180 miles round trip daily to Northwestern to complete his education and to teach.

Arthur's commitment to bettering himself through drive and hard work continued to be rewarded, not only in his day job but in academe, as well. By 1912, Arthur was appointed Assistant Professor and Head of the Accounting Department when the accounting professor holding those positions left Northwestern. By 1915, he was a full professor. With typical confidence and vision, he reorganized the department and in 1917 published his *Complete Accounting Course*. He continued to teach at Northwestern until 1922 when he resigned because his growing firm required more of his attention. He was elected to Northwestern's board of trustees in 1927 and was president of the board between 1930 and 1932. In 1941, he received the honorary law degree from Northwestern. Other honorary degrees came from Luther, St. Olaf, and Grinnell Colleges.

Most important for this story, Arthur E. Andersen was an entrepreneur. During the first half of the 20th century, there was a slow decline of family farms as people moved to the cities to work in the growing number of factories being built. The growth of manufacturing meant a rise of publicly traded companies. Those companies needed more competent accountants than were available, so independent auditing firms began to offer their services. On December 1, 1913, Andersen and Clarence M. DeLany opened a small accounting practice, Andersen, DeLany & Co. Arthur E. Andersen was only 28.

The practice that Andersen and DeLany opened had been founded by Clarence W. Knisely, who had built up a small audit practice in Chicago between 1901 and his death in 1913. Arthur E. Andersen knew Mr. Knisely and had worked with him on several accounting engagements. At Knisely's death, Andersen and DeLany purchased The Audit Company from Knisely's estate for $4,000. They took over Knisely's Chicago office on West Monroe Street, his client records, client relationships, and even the office building's maintenance staff. They had seven staff members and one secretary. They were officially in business.

There was tremendous demand for the dependable skills that Arthur Andersen's company could bring, and the Chicago office was the beginning of many other offices to come. In 1915, Andersen and DeLany established a second office in Milwaukee to be near the Schlitz Brewing Company, one of the firm's largest clients and Arthur E.

Andersen's former employer. Some of their other early clients included ITT and Palmolive.

Income tax, like Andersen, DeLany & Co., had been born in 1913, and very soon the partners added tax services to their list of offerings. Tax was initially a hook to reel in clients—the kind of clients who would also purchase audit services. But tax gradually assumed a more independent role within the firm as the new system of taxation expanded in the U.S. and became increasingly significant. To be near the Internal Revenue Service, an office was established in Washington, DC in 1921.

Andersen, DeLany & Co. was one of the earliest accounting firms to offer consulting services in addition to accounting, audit, and tax. Tax had proven to be an important client hook; investigations and business advisory services could give Andersen, DeLany & Co. an even bigger hook.[4] Many of the other accounting firms were skeptical of such a daring move. Concerned about potential conflicts of interest, George May, the head of Price Waterhouse, warned that auditors should do audits and only audits.[5] But Arthur E. Andersen confidently moved ahead, ignoring May's caution. He believed that the right people with training in his very specific methods would make the difference and set about building a workforce he could trust to do the right thing.

The firm found its employees from the growing pool of students that Andersen taught. Many came from rural communities, and most were recruited from Midwestern state colleges. In 1917, his classrooms included business and professional men who were interested in taking his new course on wartime income and excess profits taxes. Andersen found himself teaching potential clients. Many of these students were involved in the new industries created as the U.S. mobilized to enter World War I. The need for public and certified financial reporting was essential to protecting the public interest. The students, as well as Andersen and DeLany, saw opportunities in the new industries that would require monitoring and "greater publicity to the financial operations of such businesses."[6] With its credentials in accounting and expertise in audit, Andersen, DeLany & Co. stood ready to fulfill this growing need. Between 1912 and 1920, the firm grew rapidly as client billings went from $45,000 to $322,00 per year.[7]

Five years after purchasing the accounting firm, DeLany resigned. In the official histories of the firm, there is very little written about DeLany, and he is a shadowy figure in Arthur E. Andersen's life. He was a licensed CPA and had worked for Price Waterhouse before going into partnership with Arthur E. Andersen. It is likely that the two men met at Price Waterhouse when Arthur E. Andersen worked there. He may have left the partnership for personal reasons, or he may have had a falling out with his partner, Arthur E. Andersen. He resigned in 1918. One account suggests that Arthur E. Andersen did not think that DeLany fit with his vision of the firm and forced DeLany out. "DeLany was more of a bookkeeper but he was useful to Arthur Andersen at the time. He soon got rid of him," Leonard Spacek, an Arthur Andersen & Co. partner, remembered.[8] With DeLany's departure, the firm was renamed Arthur Andersen & Co. Arthur E. Andersen dominated the firm for the next 30 years.

After DeLany's departure, Arthur E. Andersen turned to his younger brother to run the Chicago office. Walter H. Andersen had joined Andersen, DeLany & Co. in 1916. In contrast to Arthur E. Andersen, who could be strict in his views[9] and had a reputation as being "often autocratic and sometimes arbitrary,"[10] Walter was kindly and personable but had a streak of independence. The differences in temperament between the brothers did not deter Arthur E. Andersen from giving his brother opportunities to succeed. Walter agreed to oversee the Chicago office and took over responsibility in 1919.

Arthur shifted his attention to building Arthur Andersen & Co. From 1919 until his death, Arthur E. Andersen oversaw the addition of offices in Kansas City, Los Angeles, New York, San Francisco, Detroit, Boston, Houston, Atlanta, Minneapolis, St. Louis, Seattle, Cleveland, and Philadelphia, as well as Washington, DC. The Milwaukee office had been opened in 1915. Although the growth of the firm was impressive, Arthur actually was careful about growth and did not want to sacrifice quality. The people acquired through the 1913 purchase of The Audit Company of Illinois from Knisely turned out not to be up to the standards of Arthur E. Andersen and couldn't be trusted to do an audit to his specifications. He replaced five of the original seven staff. Arthur E. Andersen decided that the only staff he could trust were those he trained. The only offices that would be added to the firm would be those that he would personally establish with his own people. Arthur Andersen & Co. grew slowly and carefully under Arthur's guidance.[11]

Then, in 1932, Arthur E. Andersen experienced a set back. His brother, Walter, resigned. According to Leonard Spacek, who was working in the Chicago office at the time, the two brothers got into a fight, and Arthur E. Andersen ordered Walter out of the office. The two never spoke to each other again.[12]

Arthur E. Andersen also tried to convince his son, Arthur Arnold Andersen, to join Arthur Andersen & Co. Arthur Arnold tried working for his father for a while but apparently his employment with the firm did not work out, either, and he left in 1943 after three years with the firm. Arthur E. Andersen was bright and ambitious but he was also blunt, domineering, and unforgiving.

Think Straight, Talk Straight

From the beginning of Arthur Andersen & Co., the firm used Arthur's experience, reputation, and vision as the foundation of its competitive advantage. But it was not just what Arthur did professionally that was so remarkable; it was the spirit in which he did it. Arthur Andersen could not be bought.

"Think straight and talk straight"[13] was the principle on which Arthur E. Andersen built his accounting practice. It was a phrase his mother had taught him. It became the firm's motto and appeared on many internal documents. The commitment to integrity and a systematic, planned approach to work is what he offered his clients, and this brand of audit proved attractive to both corporate clients and investors.

Within the firm, stories circulated for decades after his death about how he had done the right thing when it was *not* the only choice but when it was the less profitable or more difficult choice. In one such story, Arthur faced a client who had distorted earnings by deferring large charges, rather than reflecting them in current operating expenses. The president of the company flew to Arthur Andersen's office in Chicago and demanded he change the audit certification to suit the client's version of the truth. Arthur replied, "there is not enough money in the city of Chicago to induce me to change the report."[14] Arthur lost the client but gained something more important— a reputation for straight talking.

Another story recounts how Arthur faced up to a lucrative steam- ship company client. To help attract investors for a bond offering, the steamship company asked Arthur to certify its financial statement as of December 31, 1914. This was prior to the loss of one of the company's new ships in February 1915. Certifying the statement as of the earlier date would camouflage the company's loss and would misrepresent the real financial assets of the company to potential investors. Andersen refused to certify the financial statement without disclosing the loss.

Arthur was a realist and maintained some skepticism of client management. Auditing was founded on the idea that a company's inter- nal accounting cannot be relied on to provide the unvarnished truth. He was well aware that straight reporting meant that auditors needed to check reality and make sure that the material facts reported by the cli- ent were accurate and required that an auditor understood "the facts behind the figures." As Paul K. Knight, an early Arthur Andersen & Co. partner, explained, it is the auditor's job "to ascertain the factors that contributed to the operating results and form a business judgment as to how to improve the good factors and eliminate the bad."[15] The Andersen reputation for resisting misleading reporting and telling it like it was grew, and getting the Andersen name on your company audit became increasingly desirable.

Arthur E. Andersen took ownership of the audit and he was prepared to stand behind his work. The generally accepted position on audits the first quarter of the 20th century was that they belonged to the client. But, Arthur E. Andersen reasoned, because audit materials carry the Arthur Andersen & Co. name, audit reports should belong first and foremost to the firm, not the client. As auditor, he was obligated to determine what was in the audit. Arthur E. Andersen had all audit opinions signed in handwritten signature as "Arthur Andersen & Co." and, later, with "Arthur Andersen & Co." plus the responsible partner's name below it. If any errors or problems were found, they would be corrected, and Arthur Andersen & Co. would pick up the associated costs if the firm was at fault.

Ensuring a Quality Workforce

When Andersen and DeLany purchased their firm, people in the accounting profession were seen as low-level, bookkeepers. But Arthur E. Andersen insisted that a CPA could be much more. Auditors, he believed, had a serious personal and professional responsibility to know the facts behind the figures and to protect the public interest. Arthur E. Andersen set out to find and train a pool of reliable young men who could live up to the professional standards he set.

"The thoroughly trained accountant must have a sound understanding of the principles of economics, of finance, and of organization," he once said. "It has been the view of accountants up to this time that their responsibility begins and ends with the certification of the balance sheet and statement of earnings. I maintain that the responsibility of the public accountant begins, rather than ends, at this point."[16]

To do their job, accountants had to be well trained. Arthur E. Andersen was convinced that too many unqualified men were getting a

CPA and advocated that all accountants have an undergraduate degree to get a "broader cultural overview."[17] In 1915, Arthur Andersen & Co. became the first accounting firm to formally recruit college graduates. Arthur E. Andersen had very specific ideas about who he wanted and how he wanted them trained. He recruited impressionable young men with a strong Midwestern work ethic, just out of college, who showed intelligence but could be molded to his ideas. In addition to grades, he looked for people with modest economic and small-town or farming backgrounds. Many of Arthur Andersen & Co.'s recruits were the first members of their family to move off the farm or attend college. Over his lifetime, Arthur E. Andersen gained a reputation for finding and grooming outstanding people while keeping Arthur Andersen & Co. under his firm control.[18]

Once hired, these young recruits were apprenticed under Arthur E. Andersen or one of the other senior CPAs at Arthur Andersen & Co. Originally, aspiring accountants were required to undertake an internship as part of their training for the CPA examination. Becoming a CPA required the mastery of accounting knowledge, and it was typical for people to spend their first two years doing low-level, low-risk work under the direction of a CPA. But Arthur E. Andersen believed that it was the duty of accounting firms to provide staff with the technical tools for the job, and he required that all new staff learn and follow his methods as part of their internship.

Arthur E. Andersen may not have trusted the system that produced accountants but he had a strong belief in his own methods, and learning them became core to Arthur Andersen & Co.'s professional development. As early as 1940, the firm set up a central training program in local hotels to teach these methods. Thirty-five students attended the first week-long training, Firmwide Audit Staff Training School (FASTS).[19] The training that Arthur Andersen & Co. required was not just about helping employees prepare for the CPA exam. It was also about molding and controlling a uniform workforce that could be trusted to work to the high standards set by Arthur E. Andersen, and he personally groomed most of the men who later became early partners in his firm.

The Andersen Partnership

When Andersen and DeLany purchased their accounting practice, partnership was the established organizational structure for public accounting firms. After DeLany's departure, Arthur Andersen & Co. remained a partnership but, because he owned a majority share of the firm, Arthur E. Andersen dominated every aspect of its operation and took over 50% of all profits. In 1925, Arthur's share of profits was slightly over 57%. The firm's organizational structure very much resembled a simple pyramid with Arthur E. Andersen at the very top. The firm's structure was based not just on his majority ownership but also on his seniority in accounting and his accounting expertise. Every one of the partners who reported to Arthur E. Andersen had been carefully selected to his specifications and trained to his methods. He held command through loyalty, as well as ownership. If partners were at the top of the office pyramid, the firm's founder was at the very top of that peak. Each partner might run one of Arthur Andersen & Co.'s local offices, but Arthur E. Andersen ran the show.

In the last few years of his life, Arthur E. Andersen struggled to find a successor. His brother, Walter, had resigned from the firm in anger, and his son, Arthur Arnold, had not picked up the torch. Arthur turned to consider the partners he had groomed. One early possibility was John Jirgal, an Arthur protégé who had joined the firm in 1920. "But when Jirgal started to gain recognition in the accounting profession, Arthur banished him to the New York office and reduced his authority. Arthur E. Andersen could not bring himself to share the limelight."[20]

As Arthur Andersen & Co. expanded between 1919 and 1947, additional partners were added but Arthur E. Andersen remained fully in control, without a designated heir. He was a majority owner within the partnership and could control the outcome of any partnership vote. Even though partners did not always agree with his decisions, his was too strong and authoritative a voice to muffle.

Until the end, Arthur E. Andersen continued to hold his control over the firm's partnership. He openly stated that the partnership had to remain small to maintain the spirit of unity to speak as one firm. During his lifetime, the firm did speak with one voice—the voice of Arthur E. Andersen. Just two months before his death he continued to stress, "We must have, as we have never had before, a united family, whether the office is inside or outside of the United States."[21]

Arthur E. Andersen died in January 1947 at the age of 61. His health had been failing for some time but his death still came as a shock. On the night before Arthur was to be buried, Leonard Spacek, Arthur's protégé and firm partner, arrived at the funeral home to pay his final respects to his employer and mentor. He had convinced the funeral director to allow this late-night viewing in secret, and it was well after midnight. Against the wishes of Emma, Arthur E. Andersen's widow, Leonard Spacek had brought with him Arthur's brother, Walter. Walter and Leonard had worked together in the Chicago office and had remained friends after the unforgiving fight that had forced Walter's resignation from the firm. Since that fight, neither brother had spoken to the other. Now, Walter stood silently over the casket of his brother for several minutes before turning and walking quickly out the door. Emma "found out about it one way or another and never forgave me," Leonard Spacek remembered.[22] But Spacek was a man of integrity, and despite the widow's wishes, he believed in doing the right thing. Within days of Arthur E. Andersen's death, a bitter battle would be fought over his successor.

The Making of a Myth

After his death, Arthur E. Andersen took on a mythical stature as the firm began to celebrate its founder's life and values. Stories about his life were used to explain the Andersen culture and high standards of performance, as well as to promote a standard of beliefs and behaviors modeled on his original example. Long hours, disciplined days, and a code of conduct that existed to the end of the 20th century were the legacies attributed to the firm's founder at the beginning of that century.

Little reminders of his life and work were everywhere. An antique picture or a letter personally written by Arthur might hang in the lobby of a local office. The Andersen training center outside Chicago dedicated a section of the main building to an exhibit of his artifacts, including a pen, a ledger book, and an early time sheet. The halls of Andersen's worldwide headquarters in Chicago were lined with visual reminders too.

If Arthur E. Andersen cast a long shadow on everyday life at Andersen it was because so many aspects of his personal history, experience, principles, and values were still reflected and clearly observable to Andersen staff 50 years after his death. It is not that Andersen people went about their day thinking about Arthur—they did not—but the way his values and self-discipline were embedded in the firm's methods and ways of doing things that affected their daily lives. His example of hard work, willingness to stretch himself to the limits, and insistence on professionalism in all its forms molded daily routine. The extent to which Arthur's experiences and values were made into myth in the firm half a century after his death is a testament to the long shadow he cast at Arthur Andersen & Co.

Arthur E. Andersen's Legacies

Arthur E. Andersen governed his partnership at Arthur Andersen & Co. with a firm hand, and his ideas dominated the organizational practices that he instituted. His values were immortalized. Arthur E. Andersen's legacies that allowed the firm to grow and thrive after his death included:

1. **Integrity and Honesty**—Think straight, talk straight values that ensured the auditor's duty to protect the public established the firm's reputation.

2. **One Firm, One Voice Partnership Model**—A model for unity and cooperation that maintained control of the firm and firm values.

3. **Training to a Shared Method**—A professional development strategy to create a uniform and predictable workforce that could be trusted to do as they were taught.

Arthur E. Andersen also left the firm a Pandora's Box—consulting. He had ignored the warnings of conservative accountants that bundling consulting with audit services posed a potential conflict of interest. Arthur E. Andersen rightly believed that such a conflict could be avoided if consulting was contained. For him, the box had three sides: (1) strong values, (2) a unified partnership, and (3) staff trained to Andersen's methods.

At Andersen's trial, the firm claimed that the audit team had looked for problems but the client had hidden information from them. Whether or not this is true, Enron engaged in what is now described as "financial engineering." But the real issue on trial, both publicly and in the courts, was Andersen's legacy of honesty and integrity. To begin to look for clues that pinpoint when Andersen's Pandora's Box was pried opened, you need to learn how the Arthur Andersen & Co. partnership responded to Arthur E. Andersen's death. "I went back and read *The First 60 Years*" (a history of Arthur Andersen), said one Andersen Human Resource employee, describing her search to find answers. "It was very clear to me that the partnership was completely different back then."[23]

References

1. Arthur Andersen & Co. 1974. *The First Sixty Years: 1913–1973.* p. 5.

2. Arthur Andersen & Co. 1988. *A Vision of Grandeur.* p. 56.

3. Arthur Andersen & Co. 1974. *The First Sixty Years: 1913–1973.* p. 5.

4. Arthur Andersen & Co. 1974. *The First Sixty Years: 1913–1973.* p. 29.

5. Arthur Andersen & Co. 1974. *The First Sixty Years: 1913–1973.* p.29.

6. Arthur Andersen & Co. 1974. *The First Sixty Years: 1913–1973.*

7. Arthur Andersen & Co. 1974. *The First Sixty Years: 1913–1973.* pp. 18–24.

8. Spacek, Leonard. 1989. *The Growth of Arthur Andersen & Co. 1928–1973, An Oral History.* New York: Garland Publishing, Inc. p. 212.

9. Spacek, Leonard. 1989. *The Growth of Arthur Andersen & Co. 1928–1973, An Oral History.* New York: Garland Publishing, Inc. p. 13.

10. Arthur Andersen & Co. 1974. *The First Sixty Years: 1913–1973.* p. 92.

11. Arthur Andersen & Co. 1974. *The First Sixty Years: 1913–1973.* p. 111.

12. Spacek, Leonard. 1989. *The Growth of Arthur Andersen & Co. 1928–1973, An Oral History.* New York: Garland Publishing, Inc. p. 23.

13. Arthur Andersen & Co. 1974. *The First Sixty Years: 1913–1973.*

14. Arthur Andersen & Co. 1974. *The First Sixty Years: 1913–1973.*

15. Arthur Andersen & Co. 1970. *Behind the Figures: Addresses and Articles by Arthur Andersen: 1913–1941,* p. 13.

16. Arthur Andersen & Co. 1974. *The First Sixty Years: 1913–1973.*

17. Arthur Andersen & Co. 1974. *The First Sixty Years: 1913–1973.* p. 44.

18. Arthur Andersen & Co. 1974. *The First Sixty Years: 1913–1973.* p. 69.

19. Arthur Andersen & Co. 1974. *The First Sixty Years: 1913–1973.* p. 68.

20. Arthur Andersen & Co. 1974. *The First Sixty Years: 1913–1973.* p. 77.

21. Petersen, Melody. 1998. "How the Andersens Turned into the Bickersons," *The New York Times,* March 15, Section 3, p. 13.

22. Wartzman, Rick. "DÉJÀ VU: After WWII, Death of Founder Shook Arthur Andersen," *The Wall Street Journal,* May 1, 2002

23. Personal communication—Individual's identity has been omitted to provide confidentiality.

3

GROWTH BEFORE THE STORM

At Arthur E. Andersen's death, the partnership was thrown into a crisis. Arthur E. Andersen had hopes that his son, Arthur A. Andersen, would take over the firm after his retirement or death. But his son walked away from his father's firm in 1943, leaving him without provisions for succession. The remaining 25 partners were restricted to two choices: Disband the firm or continue it as a partnership.

Their choices were limited by federal regulation. In reaction to the crisis following the 1929 stock market crash, which touched off a long period of global economic depression, the SEC was created. In one of its first actions, the SEC moved to limit potential for conflict of interest in public accounting firms by prohibiting them from being corporations with investors. Accounting firms had traditionally been partnerships, but this made it mandatory.

The partners fought bitterly over their options. "The arguments became . . . vociferous," Leonard Spacek remembered.[1] George Catlett, who joined Andersen in 1940, added, "It was really an argument about who was going to run the firm."[2] Things became even more complicated when Andersen's son, Arthur Arnold, tried to step back in and take over. Because his father had controlling interest and the firm bore the Andersen name, he assumed that "he just inherited," Leonard Spacek said. But, of course, he had left the firm years before and wasn't a partner. He really had no place with the firm.[3] Arthur Arnold Andersen was furious and threatened to deny the use of the family name but had no grounds to pursue his attempt to step in and run the firm.

A long-standing rift between the Chicago and New York offices and the control that Arthur E. Andersen had exerted over his firm had left a deep scar on some partners. They would rather dissolve the firm than repair the rift or come under such control again. And that is exactly what they decided. They voted to break up the firm and go their independent ways. But there remained a few determined disciples who could not let the firm die with its founder. The night after the vote, Leonard Spacek and a few other partners met behind closed doors to hammer out a plan to pull the feuding partners together and lift the firm back from the brink of collapse. The next day, they called all the partners back together to offer an arrangement that could set the firm back on the road to growth and success. The solution contained some significant changes in the firm's organization and financial structures.

No longer would the firm be dominated by one man. Partners would have more real authority to run their local offices as they saw fit, and the new organization would be governed by the principle of "one partner, one vote." In the spirit of all for one and one for all, the firm unity would be maintained through partner cooperation. The firm would continue to speak with one voice but now that voice would be based on the majority wishes of its partners. The partners would all share more equally in the profits and in the debt, too. It cost $1,726,400 to purchase the founder's share of the firm, a debt that wasn't fully paid off until 1964.

To coordinate the local offices and overall operation of the firm, the partners created a seven-man advisory committee. All on the committee were Arthur E. Andersen's protégés. P.K. Knight of the New York office chaired the committee. Charles W. Jones, managing partner of the Chicago office, was elected vice chairman, and Leonard Spacek was designated administrative partner.[4]

This alternative partnership arrangement was accepted, and the partners rescinded their earlier decision to disband the firm announcing, "Mr. Andersen has left us a heritage for which we shall be eternally grateful. We will show our gratitude by carrying forward with a united spirit."[5] Once the succession crisis caused by the death of its founder had passed, the firm began to grow. The partners continued Arthur E. Andersen's founding values of honesty and straightforward communications, and the firm's motto continued to be "Think Straight, Talk Straight." Over time, it became recognized among partnerships for its size and longevity.

In hindsight, a number of people within and outside Andersen concluded that it wasn't so much corruption or greed that lead to the firm's problems with Enron. It was better understood as an unfortunate consequence of the increased independence granted to local offices during this time. Arthur Andersen had been an advocate of more centralized control with uniform standards and common procedures, rejecting the traditional concept of treating local offices as individual fiefdoms. Even so, Andersen "gave local offices extensive autonomy, especially with respect to making engagement-related decisions, but neither he nor any of his successors ever relinquished complete control to the offices."[6]

Andersen's view was that each of the firm's offices should be self-sufficient and staffed to handle the audit, accounting, tax, and systems needs of its clients. Operating under general policies and guidelines established by the partners, Andersen felt individual offices should be free to manage their own operations and responsible for their success, yet act as one firm, speaking with a unified voice. As majority owner, his voice was dominant. Even though subsequent leaders did not entirely relinquish centralized control, none after Arthur was majority owner. Some reasoned that, in reaction to the solitary rule of one strong individual, the era after its founder's death marked an evolution of slow, seemingly consistent change, not unlike that of many companies. But within that gradual change would come a drift from some of the principles that Andersen felt had to be maintained to remain credible and in control. That, some reasoned, was the ultimate cause of the firm's destruction. Certainly by granting the local offices more independence, the potential for a rogue office was increased.

Growth

Arthur Andersen & Co.'s partnership was now ready to take advantage of the post-World War II economic boom of the 1950s, and the firm expanded in the U.S. and internationally. Because the partners could operate independently on the basis of guidelines, rather than rules, Arthur Andersen & Co. was able to expand without major changes in its organization for some time. The independence of local offices also provided the flexibility to respond quickly and effectively to local business conditions. Partners could confidently send out teams of trained specialists at a moment's notice. High-quality, bright staff all working to the same set of methods was the cornerstone of Arthur Andersen & Co.'s early success and a formula for growth and profitability. It could be replicated anywhere in the world. They could hit the ground running on every continent. Using this unique formula, the firm found it had a winning combination to compete successfully against other accounting firms in the rapidly changing marketplace during the second half of the 20th century.

Leonard Spacek had a seminal experience in the 1950s that galvanized his determination to grow the firm. He was summoned to New York to meet with the heads of several firms because, as Spacek tells it, "they were annoyed with all the speeches I had been making about the need to improve accounting principles to assure realistic financial reporting."[7] The head of Price Waterhouse, George O. May, told Spacek in no uncertain terms that "the major firms decide what the principles should be," gratuitously adding, "yours is not a major firm."[8] Spacek resolved to grow the firm to the point that its voice could be heard.

The mutual support of the partnership members and the firm's strong culture helped Andersen remain stable as it grew from 1950 to 1970 to a total of 87 offices that employed nearly 10,000 people in 26 countries.[9] Half of the new offices were outside the U.S. The partnership grew first within North America before expanding into Mexico in 1955, then to Europe, South America, Asia, the Middle East, and Africa. During the same period, from 1950 to 1970, its revenues increased from $8 million to $190 million,[10] an increase that made it the second largest auditing firm, behind Peat Marwick.[11] During this period, Leonard Spacek played a pivotal role.

Only two years after the partners created the seven-man governing committee to oversee the firm, Leonard Spacek took control. Unlike Arthur E. Andersen, he did not own a majority interest in the firm and so could not use this tactic as a platform for command. Instead, he gained dominance using "equal parts of drive, obstinacy, and intimidation."[12] In 1949, the partnership voted to increase his responsibilities and gave him the title Managing Partner. Leonard Spacek continued to lead the firm until 1970.

Leonard Paul Spacek

Spacek had been one of Arthur E. Andersen's protégés, and he fully embraced the core values and work practices that his mentor had advocated. The vision he provided to the firm was his version of Arthur E. Andersen's belief in integrity and fairness. He was an Arthur E. Andersen man and perfectly fit the profile that Arthur E. Andersen sought in his employees. In many ways, he was just like Arthur E. Andersen.

He came from the small town of Cedar Rapids, Iowa, where he had been born in 1907 to Paul and Emma Cejka Spacek. His father had bought a farm outside of town but Leonard's mother became seriously ill and eventually was hospitalized for a number of years. His father's income was not sufficient to maintain the farm or care for his three sons, 8 to 13 years of age. Leonard was taken in by local farm families, where he spent his mornings and evenings working for his room and board. He continued working while he finished high school.

In 1924, when he was just 17, he accepted a job in the accounting department of Iowa Electric Light and Power Company, a client of the firm. In 1925, he completed high school and continued his education, attending college at night, and working during the day in the accounting department while also holding down an evening job. Seven days a week for two years, he worked and attended college, leaving his home at seven o'clock in the morning and returning home after midnight.

His experience in the utility industry brought him to Arthur E. Andersen's attention. He was brought in contact with the firm's personnel as it was conducting Iowa Electric Light and Power's audits. In 1928 he accepted a position as a junior accountant on the Chicago staff of Arthur Andersen & Co. and was put in charge of the firm's public utility work. Joining Arthur Andersen and Co. gave him the financial security he needed to propose to Libbie Smatlan, and they married on January 19, 1929. In the years that followed, Libbie stayed at home to raise their two children while Leonard Spacek climbed the Andersen hierarchy, becoming a manager in 1934. After he finally received his CPA, Arthur E. Andersen made him a partner in 1940. He never finished his degree at Coe College but the college awarded him an honorary Doctor of Laws degree in 1962. At Arthur E. Andersen's death, he had stepped in to save the firm from disbanding and, at 41, became the firm's second managing partner, a position he held until 1963 when he moved to the newly created position of Chairman, which he held until 1970.

During his time as Managing Partner and Chairman, the accounting profession began to grow more and more complicated. Leonard Spacek, who had shown such determination in pulling the firm together after Arthur E. Andersen's death, became a fiercely outspoken champion of shareholders rights. He wrote and spoke frequently on the subject of "fairness" in accounting, declaring in 1958 that "the man on the street... has the right to assume that he can accept as accurate the fundamental end results shown by the financial statements in annual reports."[13] Other accounting firms did not always share this attitude and he had very difficult relations within the accounting industry because of the stands he took on professional issues. "Some accountants think his position is too rigid, and the feelings toward him of the seven other [major firms] range from cautious cordiality to simmering hostility."[14]

On the 50th anniversary of the firm—December 1, 1963—Spacek stepped down as Managing Partner. He recommended Walter Oliphant to replace him after discussing with the advisory committee the merits of each of the 250 active partners who might also have been considered for the position. Oliphant was Spacek's protégé and he steadfastly supported Spacek's belief that the firm would never compromise on quality. "We all recognize that changes in the profession, the overall business environment, and now in the competitive marketplace can change a firm's emphasis and approach. But any approach that does not focus heavily on quality of service is surely foredoomed to fail."[15]

Although Walter Oliphant became Spacek's heir apparent, Spacek did not turn the reins of power over to the younger man when Oliphant became Managing Partner. Instead, he stepped into the newly created position of Chairman, which "involved no operating responsibilities, but centered around 'maintaining and advancing the firm's aggressive position in the establishment of sound accounting principles within the profession, the development of the firm's special services... and firm-wide promotional activities.'" Essentially, this meant responsibility for professional leadership, business development, and sales.[16] If Oliphant was disappointed, he never voiced it as Spacek continued to lead the firm. After all, Spacek was only in his mid-50s "and was still as exuberant as ever, so most of us just decided to keep on dancing with the one who brung us," explained one partner.[17]

In his drive to achieve unbiased accounting standards, Leonard Spacek faithfully supported Arthur E. Andersen's professional development program. Arthur Andersen & Co. poured 15–20 percent of the firm's net revenue into its professional development program, to select and train exactly the right people and to make sure it kept only the right people. Andersen's values, methods, and culture were instilled through centralized training and reinforced by local office apprenticeships. Every Andersen employee learned the necessary core values and work practices expected of all who worked there. Eventually, Andersen's professional development program was ranked #1 among corporate training programs. Over the decades, these educational and career development mechanisms became central to the firm's culture.

Spacek continued to advise and guide the firm as a Senior Partner until he retired in 1973.[18] Shortly before his departure, *Fortune* magazine declared that:

> **Arthur Andersen's differentness can largely be traced to the personality of a strong partner, Leonard P. Spacek ... who for many years has been the dominant figure in the firm. Spacek has become internationally famous, if not legendary, as a result of his attacks on the accounting profession. Although he stepped down as chief executive seven years ago, he remains intensely active, and his spirit and influence are unmistakably evident.... Top partners at other accounting firms, though they can't abide his hellraising, readily acknowledge that Spacek has a brilliant, creative mind.[19]**

Expansion

Although growth was welcomed, Leonard Spacek took a conservative approach, resisting the temptation to expand rapidly and rarely acquiring firms or using affiliation agreements to grow, as many of the other accounting firms were doing. He remembered the warnings of his mentor, Arthur Andersen, against this type of growth. Concerned about maintaining quality, he preferred to establish new offices slowly.

Arthur E. Andersen had an established system for training staff to a set of consistent methods. It was an important cornerstone of success in the past, and now Arthur Andersen & Co. turned to that method to guide the development of its international offices. As the firm grew rapidly, it used this system to groom staff and expand local offices all over the world.

Experienced partners were sent to open new offices. Although each office had the flexibility to match services to local markets, responsible partners were guided by a series of methods and standards, with detailed instruction on how to set up and manage the new offices and consolidate their leadership.

As in Arthur E. Andersen's time, the organization for all new offices was a hierarchy built on expertise[20] with a clear chain of command. The Partner-In-Charge led a team of partners to run their local business operations. Teams provided services, called *client engagements*, to the client, mostly on site in the field. Managers were on the next level down and were usually responsible for the day-to-day supervision of client engagement teams. Very large engagements would have a number of managers assigned to them. The bulk of the fieldwork was done by the rank-and-file staff who made up the majority of the workforce in the local offices and throughout the firm. Professionals were supported by administrative staff who formed the operational infrastructure of each local office. Administrative and support personnel typically did not generate fees, and it was understood that "If you were bringing revenue in, then you were a real person."[21]

The local office model used in the U.S. was duplicated all over the world, providing continuity to the local office system. When partners were sent to start new offices, they would first develop recruiting relationships with local universities, using the same college recruitment strategy used in the U.S. Local recruits were then "brought up" in the firm's culture, where prospective partners were screened, trained, and groomed.

As in the U.S., methods guided the audit process, and professional development ensured conformity to the standards set at Arthur Andersen & Co. Common training provided a way for Andersen recruits to come up to speed on engagements in the U.S. and around the world. Method was the foundation for all training. Staff joked that there was a methodology for everything and that Arthurs were so used to doing things by the book that they even went to the restroom at the same time. Arthur E. Andersen had been convinced that if all staff worked to a method, this would ensure efficient and effective work practices that would consistently deliver high-quality services. As Arthur Andersen & Co. expanded, method became the foundation for growth. There were instructions covering every aspect of work, including the firm's way to accept an assignment, make a presentation, select staff, and blend with a client culture. There was even advice on how to stretch your personal budget if you did not have much to spend on clothes. Every office included a Methodology Coordinator who was responsible for keeping everyone up to date on the latest methods for doing most tasks. Knowing the method set the standard and helped lower the risk of using inexperienced staff on a client engagement.

Method was always important for accounting and accountants at Arthur Andersen & Co. had always been methodical. Learning the methodologies was an important part of getting a start at Arthur Andersen & Co. and was the bond connecting the local offices to each other. By the late 1960s, Method/1 was introduced to make the firm's IT design and installation engagements more orderly and easier, and to help manage the large teams that the jobs required. Training programs were guided by another method, Method/E, a combination of theoretical and practical applications in the field of instructional design, coupled with a method to determine training needs and develop instruction to meet them. The Method/E and Method/1 documents each occupied a shelf several feet long.

When personality typing became fashionable, the firm adopted it as a method for staff and clients to interact more efficiently. Staff members had to identify their own personal traits and the traits of others. Style and personality typing became quite popular and, at Andersen gatherings, employees could be overheard telling a friend what their type was or asking new acquaintances for theirs. The most popular system was one called the *Myers-Briggs*, which identifies four basic personality types.

Learning methods in combination with on-the-job training made a powerful combination for ensuring a consistent workforce in all local offices. At the local office, on-the-job training was founded on a model of apprenticeship. Partners played a pivotal role in the apprentice system as firm experts and mentors. Not only did they teach at the training centers but they also acted as role models in local offices. It reinforced their status in the hierarchy. Partners mentored managers and sometimes even staff, especially in smaller offices. Senior partners, who had acquired extensive experience, especially with difficult clients and assignments, regularly provided mentoring to less experienced partners. Managers were expected to follow the partner's lead, mentoring their staff and so on throughout the hierarchy.

In the first few weeks after hire, new staff from all parts of the world were sent to learn the methods and be given an introduction to the Andersen culture. Everyone was required to attend centralized training. It was the glue that connected each independent office to the others. The classroom provided a safe place to learn what happened on an engagement and what it would be like to be sent to live and work with other team members, sometimes in places far from home. Everyone had a chance to learn how to handle themselves and others during the class activities, tests, team problem solving, role-plays, simulations, and exercises. They also learned how to tolerate each other. People were often reminded that they didn't need to like each other to work together. On the line, however, successful teams were often people who did get along well. They enjoyed their work and their colleagues' company.

It was expected that a new staff member would need about four to six years to learn all that was necessary for promotion to manager. It took about 10–12 years to make partner. Selection and promotion processes guaranteed conformity to Arthur Andersen & Co.'s standards, ensuring that everyone in the local office shared the same goals, "spoke the same language," and had the same work practices. The processes winnowed out those individuals who did not have the appropriate values and behaviors.

When growing a new office, only after a local partner had gone through the professional development process was he ready to take the reins of leadership. It sometimes required a good 15 years to get an Andersen office established in another country. Following the Andersen method and the "grow your own office" model gave numerous partners extensive international experience. One partner, involved in developing a new office in Asia, said the model had given the firm the advantage it needed to become a global. This "grow your own office" method ensured a uniform loyal workforce, too.

Arthur Androids

Andersen's professional development program was instrumental in maintaining an exceptionally cohesive and homogeneous culture within and across local offices. It produced loyal auditors who were molded to fit into the Andersen culture and adhere to the work standards that Andersen set. Instilling a shared methodology among staff was not intended to make people alike but to ensure consistency across the firm's global network of offices. Although the system guaranteed that everyone in the local office shared the same goals, "spoke the same language," and had the same work practices, it just so happened that individuals who were selected to work for the firm did well in a structured system and were suited to following rules and standards. Over time, Andersen's selection, training, and promotional mechanisms developed a homogenous workforce known as "Arthur Androids." Clients joked with Andersen staff that they didn't see how they found their coats because they all looked alike.

In Chicago, the limo drivers who spent their day ferrying Andersen people from O'Hare to the downtown headquarters or the training facility in St. Charles, Illinois called Arthur Andersen staff "Arthurs" to their faces and "Arthur Androids" behind their backs. The drivers liked to brag that they could spot an Andersen fare at the airport. To the practiced eye of a Chicago limo driver, the grooming, clothes, stance, luggage, and briefcase all gave away the identity of an Arthur Android. To the end, the firm continued to turn out a consistent, uniform set of rank-and-file employees who played by the rules and followed orders, regardless of what the orders might be.

Consulting

Not all of the Arthur Andersen & Co. growth came from establishing new local offices. Arthur E. Andersen had pioneered a strategy that bundled audit with consulting services, a strategy that many of his accounting contemporaries warned against as a recipe for conflict of interest. But it became standard practice at Arthur Andersen & Co. for audit and consulting to be presented side by side in the interests of all parties. However, by the 1930s, the market for consulting had dried up, so the warnings were moot for a time.

After World War II, the demand for consulting was renewed and the firm invested heavily in IT consulting. Leonard Spacek recognized an opportunity to expand the firm's consulting practice by developing the potential of a new technology, computers. He sent Joseph S. Glickauf, an Andersen employee who was an expert on mechanical punch-card systems, to attend a prototype computer demonstration at the University of Pennsylvania. Glickauf became an evangelist for the new technology, announcing, "We stand on the threshold of a new technological era as different from the one which we have just passed through as the industrial era differs from the agricultural age the impact of which will not only [affect] the office and the plant, but society itself."[22] A short time later, in 1952, he led a team that designed and implemented the first business applications for a computer, a payroll and a material control system at General Electric. Glickauf and his team established Arthur Andersen & Co.'s expertise in computer technologies while gaining the advantage over the other big accounting firms.

Despite the fact that the firm had built the largest management information systems consulting practice in the world by 1973, audit remained the focal point of services and power within the partnership. Although the marriage of accounting and computers was valuable to clients, some partners were reluctant to grow the consulting business and, during the late 1950s and 1960s, consulting services accounted for only about 20 percent of the firm's business.

Although Arthur E. Andersen had ignored conflict of interest warnings, some partners who followed him took a different view. They believed that the new Administrative Services Division offering technical services was at the very edge of appropriate business for an accounting firm. They believed that independent public accounting firms had a responsibility to avoid work that might make management decisions for a client, and they put limits on the work that the Administrative Services Division could do, restricting it to developing and gathering information but not making decisions.[23]

Balancing Flexibility with Control

As Andersen grew, both from international expansion and through diversification of services, its independent local offices provided the firm with the flexibility to expand. However, the firm was not designed to manage an organization of Andersen's increasing scale. Only two things kept Andersen from falling apart: its strong, shared culture of values and methods and the unity of the partnership. Without these two safeguards, the local offices would be free to do whatever they wanted—right or wrong.

During his lifetime, Arthur E. Andersen had warned the partnership to remain small—no more than 100 partners—in order to retain a unified voice. Each of the 25-member partnership remaining after Arthur E. Andersen's death knew each other personally—their strengths, their weaknesses, their aspirations. Trust was founded on personal knowledge, as well as shared ideals. Personal knowledge helped make decision making faster and easier. Although each partner was responsible for the operations of his, and later her, own office and client engagements, each also had a firmwide obligation to help others if needed. Under Leonard Spacek's 25-year guidance, cooperation and a common experience kept the partnership and the firm united.

The partners developed a self-reinforcing, informal exchange system of rewarding favors. A partner might share available staff or steer work in the direction of another partner. A staff person might help a partner with a charity or professional association event on his or her own time or take an undesirable assignment for the sake of the firm or out of loyalty to the partner. Such a sacrifice might be repaid by a high-visibility assignment and eventual promotion. Exchange arrangements helped to cement and stabilize the partnership and provided a flexible system for finding and deploying staff quickly, giving Andersen an edge over the competition.

Partners who worked well with the others could multiply efficiency and improve the bottom line. Cooperation opened doors and smoothed operations. The more staff a partner could send into the field on an engagement he sold, or on one sold by a colleague, the more money he or she could bring into the firm. The more money a partner brought into the firm, the higher the rewards were for everyone. The partner benefited on an individual level, and the partnership benefited as a group. Reciprocal exchange of resources and engagements kept the offices within the firm connected and made it successful. As the number of Andersen partners grew in pace with the growth of the firm, the partnership tried to maintain cooperation. This became increasingly difficult. By 1956, the partnership had more than tripled since the founder's death in 1947 to 85 partners. In 1973, when Spacek retired from the firm, there were 826 partners, 137 of whom were nationals of countries other than the U.S. Between 1947 and 1973, the number of local offices grew from 16 to 92.

Technical skill, hard work, commitment, and performance did not make advancement to the top automatic. Each and every partner was selected and groomed by Arthur E. Andersen's former protégés exactly as they had been selected and groomed. Prospective partners needed to show that they were clearly one of Andersen's own, fit the partner profile, and could be trusted to work for the good of the firm, as well as for their own benefit. To win acceptance and the election, a successful candidate had to demonstrate a mix of technical and personal talent.

But, as early as 1965, continued growth had Andersen's new managing partner, Walter Oliphant, worried about the possible division of the firm into geographic compartments of interest, saying, "Such divisions need not and should not occur," and he moved to improve communications between offices.[24]

But many partners weren't worried. What could go wrong? Fueled by belief that bigger must be better and encouraged by deregulation, American business was expanding rapidly in the later part of the 20th century. Andersen, especially the younger partners, wanted to get into the game. "Winning isn't everything, it's the only thing," was a favorite Vince Lombardi quote heard around the firm. Beginning in the 1970s, Andersen began to grow rapidly and, by 1978, it was already one of the top eight accounting firms in the world. But to win, Andersen had to be number one. To win, Andersen was going to have to be the biggest, most aggressive kid on the block.

When the European Union became a reality, Andersen was well established in the Union's member countries and already had an eye on the most profitable opportunities. As the Soviet system deteriorated, teams were dispatched to Russia to determine the right time to invest there. Andersen established an office in China years before other Western accounting firms began to think about doing business there. Henry Kissinger was the keynote speaker at the firm's globalization conference in 1992. Andersen had embraced worldwide growth with ease. By the time Andersen closed up shop, it was operating in 84 countries around the globe.

Leonard Spacek lived to see it all. By the time he died in 2000 at he age of 92, he had become accounting's elder statesman, who had never been afraid to say what he thought. Throughout his career, he advocated strengthening audit procedures and standardizing accounting rules so that financial statements could be fairly compared. Under his watch, Arthur Andersen had undergone worldwide growth, with revenues jumping from $8 million in 1950 to $190 million just 20 years later. And although he had been responsible for growing Andersen's consulting services, he spoke often and eloquently about the auditor's role as a protector of the public interest. "There aren't any Leonard Spaceks in the industry anymore," former SEC Chairman Levitt eulogized.[25]

References

1. Wartzman, Rick. "DÉJÀ VU: After WWII, Death of Founder Shook Arthur Andersen," *The Wall Street Journal*, May 1, 2002.
2. Wartzman, Rick. "DÉJÀ VU: After WWII, Death of Founder Shook Arthur Andersen," *The Wall Street Journal*, May 1, 2002.
3. Wartzman, Rick. "DÉJÀ VU: After WWII, Death of Founder Shook Arthur Andersen," *The Wall Street Journal*, May 1, 2002.
4. Arthur Andersen & Co. 1988. *A Vision of Grandeur.* p. 82.
5. Arthur Andersen & Co. 1988. *The First Sixty Years: 1913–1973.* p. 32.
6. Arthur Andersen & Co. 1988. *A Vision of Grandeur.* p. 35.
7. Arthur Andersen & Co. 1988. *A Vision of Grandeur.* p. 91.
8. Arthur Andersen & Co. 1988. *A Vision of Grandeur.* p. 91.

9. Arthur Andersen & Co. 1988. *A Vision of Grandeur.* p. 196.

10. Arthur Andersen & Co. 1988. *A Vision of Grandeur.* p. 196.

11. Barner, Bella. "Don't Blame Joe Berardino for Arthur Andersen," *Virtual Strategist,* Issue 4, Fall 2002.

12. Arthur Andersen & Co 1988. *A Vision of Grandeur.* p. 121.

13. *The Accounting Review.* 1958. p. 368–379.

14. Arthur Andersen & Co. 1988. *A Vision of Grandeur.* p. 118.

15. Arthur Andersen & Co. 1988. *A Vision of Grandeur.* p. 122.

16. Arthur Andersen & Co. 1988. *A Vision of Grandeur.* p. 119.

17. Arthur Andersen & Co. 1988. *A Vision of Grandeur.* p. 121.

18. Arthur Andersen & Co. 1988. *A Vision of Grandeur.* p. 134.

19. Louis, Arthur M. 1970. "A Fat Maverick Stirs Up the Accounting Profession," *Fortune,* December, New York: Time, Inc.

20. The concept of "hierarchy of expertise" is from Power, Michael *The Audit Society: Rituals of Verification.* 2001. New York: Oxford University Press. p. 87.

21. Personal communication from Audit Manager.

22. Arthur Andersen & Co. 1974. *The First Sixty Years: 1913–1973.* p. 66.

23. Arthur Andersen & Co. 1974. *The First Sixty Years: 1913–1973.* p. 64.

24. Arthur Andersen & Co. 1988. *A Vision of Grandeur.* p. 122.

25. Kahn, Jeremy. 2002. "ACCOUNTING IN CRISIS: One Plus One Makes What? The Accounting Profession Had a Credibility Problem before Enron. Now it Has a Crisis." *Fortune,* December 23.

4

LOSING CONTROL

How big can an organization become before the leadership loses control? In Arthur Andersen & Co.'s first 60 years, growth had been carefully managed through the strong leadership of Arthur E. Andersen, then Leonard Spacek. But no matter how strong the leadership is, size does have its limits. Eventually, Andersen's partners would have to face the question of control as it continued to meet aggressive growth targets through expansion of services on the international market.

But Andersen had a unique advantage that allowed it to grow ever bigger without feeling the consequences—for the time being. Unlike other accounting firms, Arthur E. Andersen had pioneered a set of shared methods that could be used throughout the firm. A common approach, in combination with the local office independence, provided the local-level flexibility to respond quickly and effectively to business conditions around the world with assurance that staff would provide quality work.

Between 1963, when Walter Oliphant became Managing Partner, to 1970, when both Oliphant and Spacek relinquished their leadership positions, the firm grew ever larger and the number of partners almost tripled—from 250 to 689 members. With a larger partnership and greater geographic distance between local offices, the partners could no longer manage the organization cooperatively or monitor their many local offices through face-to-face communication as they had done in the past. Decisions were becoming more difficult to reach and implementing them was even harder. It was common for partners to explain that directing the firm was like steering a battleship. Like the battleship that travels 17 miles before beginning the turn, once a decision to change direction was made, the firm took what seemed like forever to implement it.

But growth was the firm's expressed goal and the firm's structures would have to adapt. Ironically, the very structures put in place to reestablish control fragmented the firm after Arthur E. Andersen's death, setting loose both the local offices and consulting services.

Before Oliphant stepped down, he warned, "As we become larger and more widespread geographically, we face an increasingly difficult task to maintain the oneness in philosophy and practice that has been the foundation of our firm over all the years. If we take these strengths for granted, we will surely lose them. If we don't work at preserving them, they will erode away. By no means are they guaranteed. They are a heritage that must be kept alive."[1] He left the task of preserving the firm to Harvey Kapnick.

Like his predecessors, Arthur E. Andersen and Leonard Spacek, Harvey Kapnick was a Midwesterner. His father was a farmer in Michigan. Kapnick attended Cleary College in Ypsilanti, Michigan after high school but his education was interrupted by World War II. He enlisted and served in the southwest Pacific, where he distinguished himself. After the war, he returned to college, completing his Bachelor's degree before attending the University of Michigan's Master's program, where he studied for a year. In 1971, Cleary College awarded him an honorary degree, Doctor of Science in Business Administration. Harvey Kapnick joined Arthur Andersen & Co. in 1948 and became a partner in 1956.

Control by Division

Kapnick took over during a time of flux. Andersen was struggling to create a management structure that would accommodate its global growth and keep its independent local offices in line. But the partnership was conflicted. Local offices had always been the primary work unit of the firm and the reason for Andersen's success. No one wanted to disrupt success by reducing local office flexibility. Each office had to be allowed to retain authority for most of the day-to-day decision making. Kapnick promised to find a way to regain control of the firm, and the partners elected him to replace Oliphant based on his promise. Although he was "perhaps less visionary than Arthur Andersen, less charismatic than Leonard Spacek, less patient than Wally Oliphant, Kapnick was, nonetheless, a dynamic, aggressive, and highly successful leader" and, they hoped, "the right man at the right time."[2]

Kapnick took over leadership of the firm at a time when management science was advocating new ideas about organizations. Kapnick, jokingly called Andersen's organization man,[3] was influenced by these ideas. Kapnick's solution to the firm's growth problem was to break up the firm into manageable service divisions—consulting, tax, and audit. He also proposed transferring significant leadership functions to local-level partners by division and geographic location. The plan was a bold change for the partnership and was opposed by many who were concerned with partner unity. The partners had traditionally depended on a high level of face-to-face contact to manage the firm and to monitor local offices. Mutual knowledge of the partnership members and the firm's strong culture were the two key factors that helped Andersen remain stable as it grew: Most Andersen partners grew up in the firm's culture. They believed in the firm's values and understood the reasons for expected behavior. Most thrived in the Andersen environment, and few ever left, except to retire. The firm was like a second family. These partners worried that, under Kapnick's plan, "we cannot retain a one-firm concept with such [a divided] organization."[4]

Kapnick disagreed with the opposition. He proposed that, under his management, the new organization could even strengthen the one-firm philosophy. After all, by 1970, most partners knew only a small number of the partnership's nearly 700 members. It was so large that one partner admitted he didn't know many of his fellow partners and might not recognize one if he tripped over him in the hall. Maintaining personal relationships throughout the partnership based on face-to-face contact was not realistic, and keeping track of what partners were up to at the local office was nearly impossible. With sheer size, maintaining the unity of the partnership was becoming more and more difficult, anyway. At least under Kapnick's plan, the partners could be encouraged to work together within their division or geographic area.

Spacek, now a senior partner, supported Kapnick. At the 1970 partners' meeting, Spacek said, "Positions of leadership should be filled by nationals of a country, and the sooner we achieve that goal, the sooner we will have strong national practices and a truly integrated international organization, because roots must run deep if you are to grow a strong, healthy tree."[5]

With Spacek's support, Kapnick got his way. By 1973, Administrative Services; Accounting and Audit Services; and Tax Services each had its own division, with new partner categories and titles to reflect the shift in leadership roles and responsibilities to the three divisions. Office Managing Partner was the new title given the partner with overall responsibility for each local office. Two new partner classes were created. Country Managing Partners were given regional or geographic responsibilities, and Practice Directors developed industry or practice specialization. Along with these changes came a more complex internal hierarchy.

Division Allegiance and Individual Success

Kapnick's reorganization had two consequences. As Kapnick predicted, it created more manageable units within the firm. At the same time, as some of the opposition partners predicted, it shifted partner allegiances from the partnership to the division level, effectively dividing the one firm into three.

The partners embraced the new, more workable division structures as they discovered opportunities to build and grow their office's business by becoming important within their division or by providing more than one service line at the local office level.

Because partner cooperation had always been an important component of success at Andersen, it was not difficult to transfer cooperative arrangements to the division level. What was different was the new focus for cooperation. By reducing partner unity to pursue a common good for the firm, the divisions turned inward. Division and local office loyalties replaced common good. This was a particularly important development for the consulting division, Administrative Services. Now that consulting had its own division, they were freer to groom their own staff and grow their business as they wanted.

The accounting and technology practices at Andersen had never been compatible, and from the start, the cultures of accounting and computing were quite distinct. Traditionally, Andersen professionals were selected and developed to the firm's values and specifications. But consultants did not have the same professional standards as the accounting profession even though the firm required them to get a CPA.

The consulting division began to introduce a more aggressive model for increasing revenue by stressing client services and client satisfaction, a model other divisions first resisted but would later adopt. To build a saleable staff base, consulting partners took advantage of Andersen's professional development program to gain, train, and retain an appropriate workforce that would be attractive to clients. Some partners became very good at acquiring and developing staff who were highly skilled technically. Some developed their selling skills and had the clients. Between these two types of partners, there developed a system of favors and obligations in selling work and doing the work. Andersen became a leader in IT consulting and the largest consulting firm of this kind in the world.

A complex informal partner hierarchy developed based on rankings in this elaborate internal trading system. Some of the most powerful partners were not the most profitable but the ones with the most outstanding favors. The trading of staff and sales opportunities served as a way to redistribute different forms of wealth within the firm: work on the one hand and labor on the other. If a partner had the right staff, at the right place, at the right time, he or she could make money on intrafirm staff loans. Helping each other by staffing critical projects created reciprocal debt obligations among partners. In addition, by accepting the staff on loan, the receiving partner entered into a debt relationship with the lending partner. Partners "owed" each other large and small favors. Partners could "get points" by both loaning and borrowing staff. Lending partners could build impressive power structures without actually selling by amassing favors from partners who did sell.

Generating revenue through sales or, indirectly, through lending of saleable staff increasingly became the measure of success in the consulting division, and a consulting partner with a growing revenue stream could climb the division hierarchy. Under the trading system, two success measures began to matter—performance ranking and building networks. But consulting was a small division and did not affect the overall culture of Andersen during the early 1970s. As long as it remained a small part of Andersen's overall business, consulting's tendency to divert from the traditions of public accounting could be managed, as it had always been in the past, by folding its members into the Andersen culture.

Balancing Unity and Division

Two requirements protected the firm's values and culture: a CPA license and participation in the firm's professional development program. Obtaining a CPA license was expected of all professional staff, regardless of specialty or division, and was a regulatory requirement for joining the Andersen partnership. To strengthen the professional development program and provide unity across the divisions, in 1970, Kapnick authorized the purchase of a central training facility as part of his plans to reorganize the firm, and Andersen purchased the campus of the old St. Dominick's College in St. Charles, Illinois. Officially named the Center for Professional Education, it was commonly called *St. Charles*. St. Charles was described as the jewel in the crown of the firm and the cradle of Andersen's culture. St. Charles was not just a training center, it was the symbol of Andersen unity around the world. It showcased artwork from offices in every city and country in which the firm was based. Like the flags from each country near the Culture Center, artwork displayed the scope of Andersen Worldwide. It told anyone who looked that the firm had a unified global reach. Everyone, including partners, managers, and staff, were required to attend Andersen's training facility at one time or another to learn or reestablish links with Andersen's common culture. The facility was known as "Sing-Sing on the Fox" because no one got out of going there.

Sing-Sing on the Fox

Andersen's central training center in St. Charles, Illinois could accommodate conferences of up to 2,000 people. Buildings on the 150-acre site held offices for hundreds of Andersen training and development employees, classrooms, auditoriums, and dorms for up to 1,675 students. One of the biggest jobs of the professional development program was the formal two- or three-week basic training of new Andersen staff. Those who attended called the training "boot camp." It was a little inside joke used by the students when partners were out of hearing, although partners knew of the term and used it themselves. From offices around the world, recruits shared the same training experience that introduced them to the firm, its culture, and its methods. New hires got to know their fellow students from their own offices and from other offices, and it was at training that people formed the relationships that would become the foundation of their future professional lives. Fellow recruits might later be team members or links in networks of friends and associates.

In the central quadrangle of the St. Charles training facility were two bronze figures, statues cast by J. Seward Johnson, immortalizing the ideal Andersen employees. The clean-cut man is relaxing on a bench. His tie is loosened ever so slightly, and his arm rests on the back of the bench. The standing woman with a briefcase in her hand is bending in the man's direction as though in conversation. Her short hair curls neatly at the ends; her calf-length skirt seems recently pressed. She wears sensible pumps with just the hint of a heel. The man looks in her direction as though to answer her question. Many of Andersen's real-life staff took their lead from this couple—some began to look like them after a while.

Andersen people maintained a sense of humor about the statues and the image that they fostered in Andersen's real-life counterparts. The bronze pair was officially called *Pro-Related*, but at least one partner was heard to refer to it as "The Benchleys of Nerd Circle." Partners often went down to the statue during a break to watch the young trainees troop out of class and dress the two figures for the season. In winter, they supplied scarves, gloves, ski caps, and even coats. In summer, the statues might sport sunglasses and hats or even baseball caps. Pulling together whatever was seasonally appropriate, the trainees turned the figures into comic relief, a parody of what they were to become. The students clowned around the dressed up statues and took pictures of themselves with grinning colleagues who had made it through basic training. These statues memorialize the St. Charles experience.

Management and technical consultants introduced an element of uncertainty, even risk, into the firm's strictly controlled workforce because they did not fall under standards of the professional accounting umbrella. Despite requirements meant to establish unity across the divisions, accounting, tax, and consulting continued to become quite different and more independent of each other. Andersen's division specialization became more pronounced, and multiple identities developed within the firm. The consulting staff heightened concern about being a "good fit" with the firm, and they were extensively monitored to make sure that they matched the personnel profile and loyalty levels of other staff.

Kapnick found that the training center alone was not enough to provide unity in the firm. He reorganized once again in an attempt to rein in the activities of the divisions, particularly consulting. In 1977, a new worldwide umbrella structure, Arthur Andersen & Co., Société Coopérative, was created to coordinate the activities of the various member offices, set policy, establish and monitor worldwide quality standards, and coordinate training for all personnel. The new entity was registered in Geneva, Switzerland, and Kapnick wanted to move Andersen's central operations there but in the end, Chicago remained the firm's world headquarters. Under this arrangement, each partner became both a national partner in a specific geographic area and a partner in the Société Coopérative. Andersen immediately began crafting a common operations framework and establishing all sorts of other groups, committees, and operational mechanisms to regain central control over the firm. But the new structures that Andersen dropped on top of its local offices and divisions introduced a level of complexity that was sometimes awkward and confusing, and never really took hold at the local and division levels. The divisions were working just fine and no one wanted to make his or her business more complicated. Besides, by this time, the three divisions had already started to become very different, with diverging practices, market conditions, business needs, and potential for revenues and profitability. Local office and division-level partners reacted negatively to the restructuring and, in some cases, ignored the world headquarters altogether. Andersen was becoming a conglomeration of services, public accounting being only one of many.

Outside Threat

By 1978, Kapnick's new divisional structures seemed to be settling into place while everyone was happily ignoring the world headquarters. Splitting the firm by division had divided the partners but had not seemed to detract it from becoming one of the top eight accounting firms in the world. To stay successful, the partners could not spend time worrying about internal matters; they had to deal with a series of growing external threats to Andersen's primary service—audit.

It was a founding assumption at Andersen that if accountants maintained their integrity, followed the firm's methods, and abided by generally accepted accounting principles and standards, they would avoid liability. But, beginning in the 1960s and continuing through the 1970s these assumptions were challenged by an explosion of mergers and acquisitions in the U.S. Auditors on both sides of these transactions watched with mounting concern as the Wall Street investment bankers devised new and more creative methods to finance these deals, and corporate executives speculated on the earnings potential that might result. In many cases, these mergers and acquisitions were successful and profitable. However, if the expected earnings from a merger or acquisition were not realized, investors often asked their lawyers to seek damages. With the corporate assets of the unsuccessful companies depleted, the audit firm was often the only party left with money and became the target of lawsuits.

In 1968, the Continental Vending case, tried in U.S. District Court in New York City, set precedence for such suits brought against accounting firms. In this case, the judge issued a stunning ruling that adherence to GAAP did not exempt auditors from liability if the court found that there was a need for further disclosures. This ruling opened the door to further litigation against public accounting firms, and suits rose from 71 cases in 1970 to 140 in 1971 and 200 by 1972. Audit firms found themselves on the losing side of a lawsuit if the auditors were found to have:

1. intentionally conspired to misstate a company's financial position,

2. provided inadequate scrutiny that failed to catch an unintentional misstatement of financial position, or

3. excluded the disclosure of certain financial information.

To protect the firm from litigation, Andersen created an independent oversight group, the Public Review Board (PRB), in 1974. The PRB was given the authority to visit offices, review records, and "review the professional operations of (the) firm, including how (it was) managed and financed, the scope of (its) practice, and the quality of control over (its) work."[6] Under the watchful eye of the PRB, Andersen's auditors became very conservative about who became a client and how audits were conducted.

During the 1970s, a small utility company called Northern became a principal investor in the development of the Alaskan pipeline. When completed, that pipeline allowed Northern to tap vast natural gas reserves in Canada. In 1980, Northern changed its name to Inter-North, Inc. Over the next few years, InterNorth's management extended the company's operations beyond natural gas by investing in oil exploration, chemicals, coal mining, and fuel-trading operations. In 1985, InterNorth purchased Houston Natural Gas Company for $2.3 billion and gained control of a 40,000-mile network of natural gas pipelines, becoming the largest natural gas company in the U.S. In 1986, InterNorth changed its name to Enron.

By the end of the 1970s, at a time when Andersen was being cautious about new clients, audit revenues began to flatten. With so many mergers and acquisitions, there were fewer big companies to audit and the struggle between the giant accounting firms for clients became very competitive. By the end of the 1970s, companies were beginning to take the audit function for granted. It was part of the American business system. Andersen had been founded, and for decades was dominated, by auditors. Arthur E. Andersen had built up the audit role during the 1930s, a time when the government thought that big corporations posed a threat to freedom and needed to be reined in. External audits had become a legal requirement for publicly held corporations in 1933 and 1934 to protect the public from another stock market crash like that of 1929. In the late 1970s, people were not interested in remembering that audit was essential to protecting public investing. Audit itself was devalued in the marketplace. It was a hassle, but one of those things businesses had to do. For public accounting firms, audit was not a money-maker.

Then, in 1978, competition among accounting firms was raised another notch with the introduction of advertising. In 1978, the American Institute of Certified Public Accountants (AICPA) rescinded a ban on advertising and other forms of audit client solicitation. Fifty years earlier, the ban had been placed on the profession because the Institute had feared that aggressive competition in the accounting industry might compromise the integrity of audits. When the ban was lifted, competition became fierce. Some audit clients used competitive bidding, or the threat that they might go "shopping" to drive their audit costs down. Although large multinational companies had to have auditors capable of conducting complex audits for global organizations, there were a limited number of such large corporate clients on which Andersen could rely for the major portion of its audit business. As the revenues from audit services flattened, competition increased, and litigations loomed, Andersen's audit services—the core service of the firm—was under attack. Andersen needed to find a way to keep the firm financially stable.

Consulting to the Rescue

Expanding consulting services was a logical solution. Andersen was not the only public accounting firm to consider expanding nonaudit services during this period. Many local and regional firms in the U.S., as well as international firms, were already deriving revenue from tax, accounting, consulting, and other work that fell outside auditing. Now all accounting firms, regardless of size, were watching their audit fees shrink and were seeking to broaden their nonaudit services to compensate.

At Andersen, the aggressive sales strategies that the consulting division was using made it a viable, growing division within the firm. Andersen could offset the flattening revenue growth of audit by expanding consulting. But Kapnick hesitated. He had become keenly aware that consulting and audit services were growing apart, and he blamed the impact of rapid technical advances and the development of a large and expanding base of nonaudit clients as the cause. Consulting services' head, William J. Mueller, agreed on the rift between the two divisions but not the cause. He blamed audit staff's lack of technical understanding and confidence, and said, "By and large, relations of the [consulting] division with the audit division are getting worse, and it has to stop—right now!"[7] Whatever the reasons, it was quite clear by 1979 that the differences between the two divisions were real. To let consulting get bigger would only increase the rift. But Kapnick opposed the growth of consulting services within the firm because of another more important consideration—growing scrutiny of conflict of interest by the SEC and the U.S. Congress.

Through the 1970s, the SEC and Congressional committees had been concerned about a single firm auditing a client company's financial statements while helping that company plan its taxes or develop management information systems. Both the SEC and Congress shared a concern that consulting would compromise audit's independence and paid special attention to firms that tried it.

Although Kapnick disagreed with the view of the SEC that consulting impaired audit independence or put audit in a conflict of interest, he was concerned about how the SEC would react to further expansion of consulting services at Andersen.[8] There were rumors circulating that the SEC was about to propose a review of each accounting firm's audit and nonaudit fees to decide whether it was independent. If *any* audit client failed the test, the accounting firm would be asked to divest itself of consulting. Because Arthur Andersen derived more income from nonaudit than any other firm in the world, Kapnick was pretty sure the firm would be asked to get rid of consulting if it came to the test.

Kapnick was spurred into action. He went into the 1979 annual meeting of 1,100 partners with a restructuring plan that would split consulting from the firm, or as he put it, "turn one great firm into two great firms." This was exactly the opposite of the plan that the partnership wanted or had expected, and they greeted the plan with skepticism. How could Kapnick even suggest spinning off the highly successful, fast-growing consulting practice at a time when audit revenue growth was flattening? One shocked member voiced the objections that the others were thinking, asking how Kapnick could possibly make the suggestion to carve off one-third of the firm and suggested that, in his opinion, Kapnick was making an expedient choice, rather than pursuing the best possible solution. Others questioned how accurately he had read the responses of the SEC to the firm's constant argument that limiting the services a firm could offer its clients was not necessary and of benefit to no one. For the first time in memory, shouting disrupted the meeting as partners jumped to their feet to shake their fists at Kapnick. Wondering what they had gotten themselves into, newly elected partners asked, "Are *all* the annual meetings like this?"[9] Cooler heads took Kapnick aside during a break in the arguing to urge him to withdraw his proposal, suggesting that he might want to conduct further meetings with regulators or other government officials to make sure he really understood their position and that the next time he went to meetings with SEC officials or members of Congress, maybe he should bring other partners with him. Kapnick was annoyed and not about to change his mind. He refused to withdraw his proposal but he stopped short of pushing for a vote by the partnership. In the days that followed, the firm was immobilized amid the continuing controversy. Kapnick had misjudged the partnership badly. He had failed to understand fully how anxious the partners were about the continued success of the firm or how disruptive his proposal to divide the firm would be. On October 14, 1979, Kapnick resigned as chairman-chief executive, ending his duties as head of the firm as he had begun them—in controversy. A few days after he stepped down as head of the firm, he retired, saying "Since I now more clearly recognize the direction the partners wish to take in resolving the problems created by the [SEC regulations on the performance of nonaudit services by public accounting firms], I find it impossible for me to properly discharge the responsibilities of chairman and chief executive because I disagree with such course of action," adding "I have concluded that 10 years is about the maximum that a person can give to the heavy and demanding responsibilities of leading a worldwide professional organization."[10]

Andersen had been founded, and for decades was dominated, by auditors. But profits could be made in consulting and could stabilize the firm during a rocky time of litigation, competition, and decreasing audit revenue growth. Besides, Andersen had always had a technology-consulting niche and had experience managing consulting services without conflict of interest. The partners believed they could handle the risk now. With Kapnick gone, the decision to grow consulting, not get rid of it, was made. In 1980, the firm reorganized once again. This time, there would be only two practice divisions—Management Information Consulting Division (MICD) and Accounting, Audit, and Tax Division (AATD), the firm's traditional services. A third division provided internal support and management services. Consulting was on its way to becoming co-equal and would in the decade to follow eclipse the traditional accounting services that the firm had always provided. But Kapnick's solution to divide the firm by service divided the partnership and the firm's single culture. Divided, the firm would never again have complete control over its divisions and local offices. With a partnership divided, the consulting division was free to go in its own direction, elevating the value of client service—a shift that would eventually have important implications for client relationships and the sales role of partners as this new stress on service and, by extension, sales spread to the rest of the firm.

In June 2002, just two months after Andersen was convicted of wrongdoing in a federal court, Harvey Kapnick died unexpectedly at age 77. His son commented about his father, "He had long believed that the dilution of standards at his beloved firm could be traced to the rise of auditor-salesmen and the poisoning effect its drive for profits had on Andersen's famous independence."[11] Kapnick's attempt to maintain control at Andersen failed and cost him his job. He never fully realized that his plan for restructuring the firm would undermine the standards he held so dear. In a little less than 10 years, consulting would take matters into their own hands, rising up and sending Andersen into its final spiral.

References

1. Arthur Andersen & Co. 1988. *A Vision of Grandeur.* p. 140.
2. Arthur Andersen & Co. 1988. *A Vision of Grandeur.* p. 134.
3. Whyte, Jr., William H., 1956. *The Organization Man,* New York: Simon and Schuster, Inc.
4. Arthur Andersen & Co. 1988. *A Vision of Grandeur.* p. 139.
5. Arthur Andersen & Co. 1988. *A Vision of Grandeur.* p. 140.
6. Arthur Andersen & Co. 1988. *A Vision of Grandeur.* p. 137.
7. Arthur Andersen & Co. 1988. *A Vision of Grandeur.* p. 153.
8. Arthur Andersen & Co. 1988. *A Vision of Grandeur.* p.151.
9. Arthur Andersen & Co. 1988. *A Vision of Grandeur.* p.151.
10. Arthur Andersen & Co. 1988. *A Vision of Grandeur.* p. 151.
11. McRoberts, Flynn. 2002. "Repeat Offender Gets Stiff Justice," *The Chicago Tribune,* September 4.

5

CONSULTING REVOLUTION

Despite the SEC's belief that consulting posed a conflict of interest to the independence of audit, in 1979, Andersen's partners opted to expand their consulting services to offset audit's lackluster performance and to continue Andersen's growth. It was a hard choice—split out the consulting part of the firm or keep it. But competition among accounting firms was increasingly aggressive as audit revenue growth flattened. Some people might argue that the firm had no choice at all but to expand consulting, given the business and regulatory environment at the time.

The choice carried responsibilities. Independent public accounting firms had a duty to stay clear of work where their staff might make management decisions for a client.[1] From the start, Andersen's consulting division had been restricted to developing and gathering information that could *help* make management decisions but could *not make* those decisions.[2] Believing safeguards were in place, growing Andersen's consulting services appeared to be a natural and safe progression for the majority of partners, and they moved to expand the roles and responsibilities of the consulting division. Duane R. Kullberg was elected Andersen's new Chairman-CEO with a landslide vote of 96 percent on February 25, 1980. It would be Kullberg's responsibility to oversee the expansion of consulting services while moving to ease the tension within the firm that the decision to grow had caused.

In his first official speech to the partnership, Kullberg announced that he would begin by reestablishing unity within the partnership, but he also gave the nod to consulting by stressing the primary importance of client service. "Our challenge," he said, "will be to motivate our people to continue working together in our traditional one-firm spirit to assure ongoing progress in the quality of our service to clients and in our ability to see and respond to new service needs while they are still in the emerging stage. To the extent that we are able to meet that challenge, we will continue as leaders, and we will continue to grow and create new opportunities for our people."[3]

Information technology consulting was fulfilling the potential Joseph Glikauf and Leonard Spacek had predicted in the 1940s and early 1950s. By 1983, consulting revenue helped Andersen take the lead as the number one accounting firm in the Big Eight, replacing Peat Marwick. It was now the largest public accounting firm in the world, and it seemed that the partners had made the right choice. Andersen added more consulting services. With new services supporting corporations, such as strategy development and change management, came the need for staff with management consulting skills, with which Andersen could compete with firms such as McKinsey & Co. and Booz Allen. Although the partners made sure to minimize external threats from the federal government and SEC, they did not anticipate the subtler threat that consulting itself posed.

In 1979, the number of consulting employees was relatively small, compared with the rest of the firm, and traditional audit, accounting, and tax services accounted for well over 70 percent of all revenue. Auditors remained firmly in control of the partnership. However,

Andersen's consultants had autonomy as a separate division and, for some time, had been allowed to develop their own distinctive subculture. With dramatically rising revenues and an increased employee base, within just a few years consulting was in a better position to grow more than its services—it could grow its influence.

How could the partners during the 1950s have anticipated that consulting's ranks would expand enough by the 1980s to build a powerful base that could challenge the foundations on which Andersen had rested for the last 65 years? But, of course, that is exactly what happened. One by one, the consulting partners began to question the values and institutions of the Andersen culture; then they began to change them.

Consulting Challenge

Everyone was taught that Andersen's culture was the glue that held the worldwide organization together. Andersen's culture and values provided that invisible framework that allowed its decentralized local office system to work. Employees could make decisions and feel confident that their choices were consistent with the firm's principles and standards. But Andersen's culture was a culture based on the professional standards and work patterns of public accounting. After all, Andersen's core service had always been auditing, and auditing at Andersen was about method and following the rules.

But the accounting values that Andersen's audit staff understood, without comment or question, were not so easily transferred to consulting. With their own division, consulting partners were ready to establish their own brand and compete with big corporations such as IBM and Electronic Data Systems (EDS). At the center of consulting's business success was its ability to generate fees, maintain staff chargeability, and ensure client satisfaction. These did not always mix well with protecting the public's interest. Consulting was in a fundamentally different business, and most of their engagements had nothing to do with public interest. As Andersen Consulting set about building its own brand, it recruited a new type of employee who was innovative and entrepreneurial. They were not accountants and did not share the professional standards and values of the profession.

As consulting grew, its members began to challenge Andersen's core culture. Most of these challenges were innocent attempts to adapt the Andersen culture to the consulting division. The stir surrounding Andersen's double-door symbol is a good example of this type of challenge. A pair of closed doors had come to symbolize the firm during the 1950s, and the same doors were installed in local offices around the world, printed on cards, and crafted into lapel pins. They were Andersen's symbol of integrity and confidentiality. Initiated by members of the consulting division, one Midwestern office broke with tradition by installing glass rather than mahogany doors, despite considerable resistance from accounting, audit, and tax partners. The story was always told with a sense of shock. To many, it was a symptom of the growing rift between the two business units.

Other challenges were more direct. When Andersen's partnership did not go along with some of consulting's more disruptive requests, the consulting division partners could become aggressive. Under the leadership of Gresham Brebach, the consulting division staged one of several revolts to become a separate firm. But the partners, dominated by audit, rejected the idea as they had in 1979. In defeat, Brebach was fired and went on to join one of Andersen's competitors, Saatchi & Saatchi.

Incidents like the story of the glass doors and Brebach's revolt highlight the distinctions between the two groups, each with its own business needs, values, and activities. Although consulting services were too lucrative to let go, these skirmishes raised the level of anxiety. The mechanisms that maintained unity within the firm were in jeopardy.

Aware of the growing threat to Andersen's common culture, Kullberg brought in Terrence Deal, co-author of the book *Corporate Cultures,*[4] to help assess the state of Andersen's culture and its 10 core values:

1. **Client Service:** Delivering quality without compromise

2. **Hard Work:** Being responsive and timely

3. **One Firm Concept:** Many independent nationals with common objectives

4. **Recruiting Quality People:** The first major firm to do campus recruiting

5. **Training and Development:** Leadership in professional development

6. **Meritocracy:** People are rewarded based on their own merits

7. **Integrity:** Objectivity in all that we do, without fear or favor

8. **Esprit de Corps:** Pride in the organization and in belonging to it

9. **Professional Leadership:** Acknowledged leader throughout our history

10. **Stewardship:** Making long-term decisions to benefit the Firm

To Kullberg's relief, in 1986, Andersen received a positive report assuring the firm that its culture remained strong and consistent from personnel level to personnel level, from office to office, and from country to country. The firm might be geographically decentralized but it remained united by its shared culture and values. But the study also found internal tensions because the 10 formally stated values sometimes came in conflict with the informal messages that staff were hearing from the partners, particularly in the consulting division. Tension was particularly intense around Andersen's traditional value of client service. Although important to everyone, pressures to generate revenue and increase profitability confused the meaning of client service. And who was the client anyway—the public or the corporation? Maintaining local office autonomy was conflicting with Andersen's need to manage its now enormous worldwide firm through standardized policies and procedures. Conforming to rules and regulations, so important to audit, was not compatible with consulting's need for flexibility.

Among the partners, the value system was summarized into four cornerstones—client service, quality audits, good staff, and profits. The tensions that were reported convinced many partners that a serious shift in the firm's value system was in process. Some partners began saying that the four cornerstones had become "three pebbles and a boulder." The boulder was profit. But there were no easy answers. Despite the rhetoric that Arthur Andersen & Co., SC remained "one firm, one culture," this had not been true for some time.

Shifting Values

Arthur Andersen partners recognized the growing differences between the two sets of staff and tried to bring the new consultants in line with Andersen's accounting values and regulatory requirements by initially expecting every new hire to work for a time under an audit partner, become a CPA, and gain experience on audit engagements. Many consultants in the firm describe these additional requirements as "growing up with the auditors." They didn't always like it, but they went along with the requirement to meet the regulatory requirements set by the SEC for public accounting firms. Under those requirements, a person without a CPA could not become a full partner in a public accounting firm.

Another way that Andersen tried to deal with potential divergence from its core values was through its professional development program. Education had been an important and successful strategy in the past. Education was promoted as a strategy that could minimize differences now. But nonaccounting staff had problems with Andersen's rigid professional development program. One attempt to standardize management across the divisions was the Model-Netics Program. Model-Netics was a system of 152 management models—each model had a graphic symbol to help with memorization. Partners believed that by adopting the Model-Netics system, all professionals, regardless of division, would use a common management framework for communicating, managing, and decision making. After one particular training event, a workbook was left behind by one of the students. In it were several penciled notes. At the bottom of one page, a hatchet had been drawn next to a model with the penciled addition "The Hatchet, an effective tool to help uncontrollable staff better define and pursue their appropriate career paths."

However, the biggest mismatch for consulting staff was Andersen's long-established promotion process. To make sure all its employees could be relied on to follow the rules, Andersen had traditionally grown its own staff, hiring green recruits straight out of college with little or no work experience, then training the new hires to Andersen methods. But recruits with engineering, computer, and management consulting talent arrived at Andersen with specific skills and expected to use their skills once hired. Instead, they were assigned grunt work at the bottom of Andersen's hierarchy as though they were young, inexperienced accounting recruits. They were then expected to work their way slowly up the promotional chain. This treatment made no sense to ambitious, skilled professionals, particularly those with previous work experience. Many experienced hires had held important positions in other settings and knew the slow pace for promotion was not the only or even the most common method for recognition and advancement, especially to the degree found in Andersen. Consulting was also finding it difficult to retain good staff under Andersen's accounting culture.

Everyone learned that promotion to partner was uncertain, and consultants saw no reason to wait so long. Others simply could not see a career path for themselves at Andersen under any circumstances. But people with the appropriate skills and knowledge were in short supply, and demographic forecasts indicated available mid-twenties college graduates would continue to drop through the 1990s. Qualified staff could snag well-paying positions in other big firms, and other companies were happy to compete for Andersen's talent. They often paid more, too. The turnover rate among consulting staff was high. Consulting partners openly began to ask for modifications in Andersen's recruitment and promotion criteria to better reflect the business realities and work practices of consulting services.

Compromises were made. Time to promotion was shortened, and candidates could be fast tracked. Training course development was turned over to the divisions. Training was even decentralized, with facilities established in Europe and Asia, although the firm continued to require employees to attend some training at the main facility in St. Charles, Illinois to preserve that common experience. Changes to the recruiting process, the centralized training model, and career path might seem like tinkering to some but these were components of Andersen's most deeply held processes, and implementing even modest changes could have unintended consequences for the entire organizational culture, especially an organization as decentralized as Arthur Andersen & Co., SC. These adjustments undermined the Andersen culture—the glue that held the firm together. Andersen was becoming two firms with two distinct cultures and two sets of very different staff. A story told by a training evaluator at the St. Charles facility makes this point.

At the end of training, all courses were evaluated. Typically, participants were asked to fill out a multiple-choice survey at the end of their last class. The departing students were asked to check a box next to the choice that best reflected their answer to each of several questions on the survey. After one such class, an evaluator was heard chuckling in her office. On the desk in front of her were two large piles of completed surveys. On her lap were several more. She would hold a survey up in front of her at arm's length and then add it to one of the two piles. Then she would laugh. After watching this for a few minutes, a colleague finally interrupted her, asking what was so funny. "I can tell whether the student was from accounting or consulting by the handwriting," she bragged. "Look!" She held up a survey and explained. "This is a survey completed by a consulting staff person. See how the box next to their answer has been boldly checked? No staying in the lines for these guys." Her colleague nodded. Next she held up a survey completed by an Andersen accountant. At first her colleague was not sure that the survey had been completed at all. On close inspection, he could see that there was a tiny check mark neatly inserted into the small box. Both evaluators smiled. Accounting was about doing it right and following the rules. Consulting was about thinking outside of the box and making the rules. These differences were symptomatic of the diverging cultures and shifting values taking place.

Women at Arthur Andersen

Women had always worked for the firm as administrative support personnel, but until the 1980s, Andersen was not only dominated by "white" Americans, it was also almost entirely male. With growth and diversification, women began to enter Andersen as staff, move through the promotional system to manager, and, less frequently, complete the process by becoming partners. Accounting in the U.S was traditionally a male occupation, and the networks that Andersen used to recruit and educate their staff also predisposed it to a network of men. Women were just not recruited, and there was no reason to do so. Private partnerships, such as Andersen, were exempted from Equal Employment Opportunities legislation.

By the 1980s, worldwide growth created a demand for smart, skilled workers with a variety of backgrounds. Women were more likely to pursue a career in business, accounting, and computer science, so women began to be hired. But it was a difficult fit into a system that had been about male-to-male loyalty. Some partners adjusted their expectations and behaviors to include women in their offices but the more old-fashioned partners could not seem to accept women in positions beyond that of secretary. Many even hesitated to give women much time and attention, for fear it would be misconstrued as an affair. In general, women had difficulty climbing the Andersen hierarchy. Those women who were lucky enough to succeed did so by finding a way to join one of Andersen's male-dominated networks. Those who could not find a way around perception barriers left Andersen in frustration. Although the firm was recruiting 50 percent women by the mid 1980s, by 1999 only 7.5 percent of partners were women.

Partners justified the small overall number of women partners by pointing out that the long hours and high demands placed on Andersen employees made it hard to balance a career at Andersen with marriage and child care. Although this may have been true for some of the women working in the firm, it is also true that the male-oriented workplace put many women at a disadvantage and shut them out of opportunities that their male counterparts enjoyed. Ambitious, disillusioned women were more likely to leave Andersen for another job than to start a family. Eventually, women did win election to the Andersen partnership but they remained underrepresented in the U.S. and in many other countries where Andersen had offices. Women from countries such as the Philippines succeeded where their counterparts in the U.S. continued to struggle. By the end of the 1980s, Andersen was taking the presence of women more seriously and established Growth and Retention of Women (GROW) to balance the numbers and roles of women. GROW was one of the early efforts to be abandoned as events associated with Enron unfolded.

Consulting Revolt—Consulting Coup

Consulting became a full-fledged, competing cultural system that sought equality with accounting. Between 1984 and 1989, consulting's revenue contribution to the firm became significant while audit's proportion of revenues dropped (see Table 5.1). By 1989, the consulting division was on its way to contributing half of the income of the firm. As their power grew, consulting partners felt empowered to make more demands to support their business.

TABLE 5.1   Andersen Revenue Growth from 1984 to 1989.

Year	Total Firm Revenue (thousands)	Audit Revenue (thousands)	Consulting Revenue (thousands)	Tax Revenue (thousands)
1984	1,387,947	702,900 (51%)	391,800 (28%)	293,200 (21%)
1985	1,573,883	767,100 (49%)	477,300 (30%)	329,500 (21%)
1986	1,924,006	903,700 (47%)	635,900 (33%)	384,400 (20%)
1987	2,315,769	997,900 (43%)	838,400 (36%)	479,500 (21%)
1988	2,820,412	1,708,000 (60%) (Includes Tax Revenue)	1,112,000 (40%)	(Combined with Audit Revenue)
1989	3,381,900	1,940,200 (57%) (Includes Tax Revenue)	1,441,700 (43%)	(Combined with Audit Revenue)

Keeping the growing discontent within Andersen a secret was becoming more and more difficult. After Arthur E. Andersen's death, Andersen's partners had agreed to present a unified voice to the public, and partners kept their differences behind closed doors like the closed doors that represented the firm. The disagreements within the partnership were becoming so acrimonious that some accounting partners began to accuse consulting partners of being disloyal to the firm and its values. Name calling even spilled over into the local offices, where consultants began to routinely call their accountant colleagues "pencil heads," and where accounting staff responded by calling the consultants "gear heads." Over a period of time, Andersen's one partnership voice was damaged as it became impossible for the partners to contain their conflicts within their own circle. Eventually, these spats became public.

Andersen was not the only firm dealing with the tensions associated with the growth of consulting. "Accountancy may be becoming a little too exciting for its own good," noted an article in *The Economist*, pointing to sources of friction between accountants and consultants over compensation, firm structure, and access to capital. "Given the disparate rates of growth and the divergent outlooks for accounting and consulting, it's small wonder that tensions are beginning to emerge throughout the profession. Although internal spats at Arthur Andersen and Arthur Young & Co. were the first to hit the headlines, the two Arthurs are by no means alone in grappling with the accounting/consulting issues."[5]

At stake was much more than compensation. Although getting a bigger slice of the profits would be nice, the real goal was something that consulting had been lobbying to obtain since Gresham Brebach's revolt—to gain its independence from accounting. Because there were so many more accounting partners in the firm's partnership, they dominated the power structure and controlled the majority vote. Consulting partners felt powerless and were insisting on more autonomy in order to address their very different business needs.

In the end, the conflict between accounting and consulting centered on the issue of money and power. Of the 2,134 members in the partnership in 1989, only 586 were consulting partners, yet the consulting division was bringing into Andersen 43 percent of all revenue. That meant that each consulting partner was generating considerably more revenue than his or her accounting counterpart. In 1989, the average partner revenue for accounting partners was $1,415,200, whereas consulting per partner revenue averaged $2,332,800. Based on per-partner revenue contributions, consulting felt it deserved more of the financial rewards because its partners were contributing so much more than the accounting partners. Consulting partners wanted more representation on the board of partners and committees. But accounting partners claimed that the figures used by consulting were faulty. If revenue from all accounting professionals was included, the average for each accounting professional would be $93,300 whereas it would be only $79,500 for each consulting professional. The arguments went back and forth.

Ultimately, however, reorganization was necessary to realign consulting's identity and direction separate from accounting. Business demand for consulting services was increasing, and other companies, such as EDS and IBM, were gearing up to compete in the consulting market.[6] From 1987 through 1989, Andersen found itself in a major restructuring—a restructuring that would finally give consulting partners the autonomy they wanted. Higher compensation was important, Kullberg conceded, "but we could have modified the compensation plan without reshaping the organization. The fact is that the change stemmed primarily from a need to position ourselves more strategically to serve a changing market."

Consulting services changed from a division within Andersen to an independent business unit—Andersen Consulting. Andersen Consulting was now an independent entity no longer as directly under audit partner control. The Accounting, Audit, and Tax Division continued under the name Arthur Andersen & Co. To maintain the links between the two businesses, the firm kept its umbrella-like organization, Arthur

Andersen & Co., SC, which subsequently became Andersen World-wide, SC.

The two new business units set up understandings that would guide their future together. Foremost, they agreed to split the books. Now, accounting and consulting could track all income, expenses, and profits separately. Partners also agreed to a revenue-sharing formula to determine partner compensation according to an equalization formula that allowed for transfer payments of 15% in either direction, depending on whose revenues were higher. At the time of this agreement, consulting revenues still represented less than half of the firm's total revenue, so Andersen Consulting benefited from this revenue-sharing agreement. Arthur Andersen partners saw it as a continuing investment in growing consulting. Arthur Andersen also agreed to stay out of the lucrative consulting markets serving large businesses, and Andersen Consulting promised not to engage in any consulting projects for small to medium clients with less than $175 million in annual company revenue.

With the announcement of the reorganization, Duane Kullberg stepped down as head of the firm. He was replaced by Lawrence A. Weinbach as Managing Partner-Chief Executive to head Andersen Worldwide, SC. Weinbach was an auditor with a specialization in mergers and acquisitions who had joined Andersen after being educated at the Wharton Business School. Because Weinbach was based in New York, staff joked that the new CEO was "virtual" and that headquarters was wherever in the world the leader was. It would be Weinbach's responsibility to oversee the new arrangements. He announced optimistically that the new structure adopted by Andersen would become a model for global professional services firms, noting that the competitive environment in which Andersen found itself required the firm to remain flexible and alert to opportunities for growth, including the addition of new strategic business units.

Richard L. Measelle, a Midwesterner, was elected as Managing Partner for Arthur Andersen. Richard Measelle was the only one of the three managing partners to work full time at the downtown Chicago headquarters. He supported Weinbach's optimism, adding, "Serving emerging client needs is the source of [Andersen's] growth in both revenues and profitability. This also lies at the heart of [the firm's] continuing drive to diversify and expand our range of services." At the same time that Measelle was justifying Andersen Worldwide's two new business units, he stressed his strong commitment to the audit partner's role as trusted business advisor, saying, "Despite all of the changes, ...one constant remains: Auditing is the heart of our business. Objectivity and integrity, the key values that the auditor brings to his or her work, pervade all that we do."[7]

George T. Shaheen, also a Midwesterner, became the Managing Partner for Andersen Consulting. Technically, Shaheen was also based in the Chicago office, but he continued to live in Silicon Valley in California—well placed on the West Coast to court the new economy companies. (When Shaheen was in Chicago, his office was initially right next door to Richard Measelle's. But there were such tensions between the two men that, when the offices were remodeled, they arranged to be on different floors.) He set five goals for Andersen Consulting: (1) retain strong industry and business skills while deepening market penetration; (2) stay at the leading edge of information technology; (3) develop strategic, change management, and systems services; (4) invest in the new systems integration practice; and (5) achieve recognition throughout the world marketplace.

Once restructuring was completed in 1989, Andersen Consulting revenue jumped to $1,441,700 million—a 30% increase over 1988. The two business units set off on very different paths.

Management responsibilities at the local office level were split by business unit, as well. Some smaller offices and those that had good relations between the partners remained consolidated, despite the creation of two firms. But the new structure allowed Andersen Consulting to physically separate from Arthur Andersen at the local office level, and some did, establishing separate office facilities. This meant that there could be, and often was, more than one "local office" in any one city, sometimes causing great confusion among the local businesses.

A year after the restructuring, the SEC recognized Andersen Consulting as a separate entity, and Andersen Consulting was set free from many of the restrictions placed on public accounting firms. One of the first things that nearly 800 Andersen Consulting partners and managers did was to turn in their CPA licenses. They had all obtained the CPA license as a requirement for making partner. But to many of them, a CPA license had never made sense for a consultant, and it didn't make sense now.

Free to be different, Andersen Consulting moved to distinguish its individualized culture and its own identity. Andersen Consulting launched a massive $10 million advertising campaign to establish its new identity in the marketplace, kicking off the campaign with an ad running on Super Bowl Sunday.

Believing that core values were the essence of culture and drove behavior, Andersen Consulting partners convened a work group in 1992 to determine its own core values and create a new identity. What Andersen Consulting understood about culture was that it existed and was unique to each organization, was socially constructed, gave meaning to events and symbols, and guided organizational behavior. New heroes needed to be identified and a new learning organization created. As a baseline, Andersen Consulting used Arthur Andersen's 10 values. Rather than simply produce a list of values with appropriate definitions, the group took a very practical and reflective look at the real day-to-day differences of Andersen Consulting's business, business environments, and people, and made adjustments. They considered what they wanted to retain, what they wanted to delete, and what they wanted to add. After much evaluation, analysis, and discussion, the worldwide teams proposed a set of six new core values for Andersen Consulting.

1. Quality client service

2. One firm under Andersen Worldwide

3. Stewardship

4. Best people

5. Respect for individuals

6. Integrity

Some of the values were shared between Arthur Andersen and Andersen Consulting, but there were subtle differences in interpretation. There was a shared belief in client service, but a difference in how it was defined and delivered. For Arthur Andersen, Client Service had always meant service to the investing public—the stockholder. For Andersen Consulting, Client Service meant providing quality service to the people who purchased the services. Typically, corporate management hired Andersen Consulting.

The One Firm value remained the same, as did Stewardship and Integrity, but it had different meaning for consultants than for public accountants. At Arthur Andersen, the one firm included the family of services under the Andersen Worldwide, SC organization. Andersen Consulting considered the one firm to be Andersen Consulting. Stewardship and Integrity had traditionally been the watchwords for Arthur Andersen's responsibility for the public trust. Although Andersen Consulting continued to value Integrity and Stewardship, it had no such direct obligation to the public because they were not accountants.

There were also revisions that centered on several broad differences. Everyone supported playing on the #1 team and the belief that they were the best. But the Best People were different at Arthur Andersen and Andersen Consulting. In a climate of uncertainty, Andersen Consulting needed to recruit and retain good people who could respond rapidly and creatively. As a division within Arthur Andersen & Co., SC, consulting had seen its best staff leave rather than wait years for promotion or lose their home lives and relationships as casualties to long hours at the office.

The value of Hard Work for its own sake was starting to appear dated. Working smart was the new watchword. If consulting staff were to work hard—which they did—they preferred to think of themselves as road warriors, as reflected in the lifestyle of the technology sector. It was a lot more attractive and implied recognition of their value as individuals.

To reflect the different needs and expectations of the Andersen Consulting staff, the Best People value consolidated Arthur Andersen's values of Recruiting Quality People, Training and Development, Esprit de Corps, and Meritocracy.

The value of Professional Leadership was another area where the two firms had different responsibilities. Arthur Andersen was an active leader in setting government regulation and standards in the accounting industry, acting on a belief in values that transcend immediate issues and needs of the firm. Andersen Consulting sought technical leadership.

Of all the changes needed to recruit and retain the best people, the one that made all the difference was Respect for Individuals. Andersen Consulting staff expected a greater level of respect for their overall careers and a higher level of recognition of individual needs and capabilities than Arthur Andersen had traditionally displayed. Respect for Individuals reflected an important difference in spirit between Arthur Andersen and Andersen Consulting (see Table 5.2), and it was an important addition to Andersen Consulting's core values.

TABLE 5.2   Comparison of Values

Arthur Andersen's Values	Andersen Consulting's Values
Client Service	Quality Client Service
Hard Work	
One Firm	One Firm
Recruiting Quality People	Best People
Training and Development	Best People
Meritocracy	Best People
Integrity	Integrity
Esprit De Corps	Best People
Professional Leadership	Best People
Stewardship	Stewardship
	Respect for Individuals

Conflict of Interest

Arthur Andersen's common culture and shared values were coming unglued. They were geographically divided by growth in the 1960s and 1970s, and divided by division in the early 1980s, then divided into separate business units in 1988. In the 1990s, the firm found its culture and values divided as Andersen Consulting and Arthur Andersen began to move in different directions and to lead separate lives. It was clear to many partners that the firm's restructuring in 1988 was just the first step in the eventual dissolution of the economic connections between Arthur Andersen and Andersen Consulting. As the relationships among the partners steadily deteriorated through the 1990s, Arthur Andersen pursued strategies intended to put its part of the firm in a position to offset the potential loss of Andersen Consulting's economic contribution. At the same time, Andersen Consulting jettisoned the burden of public accounting firm requirements.

Although consulting and accounting were separated into two business units, this separation did not stop the infighting. In the 1990s, Andersen Consulting began to generate far more revenue than Arthur Andersen. In accordance with the agreement between the two business units, consulting now began to transfer 15% of its annual revenue over and above that of Arthur Andersen to Arthur Andersen's partners. By 1999, the transfer from Andersen Consulting partners to Arthur Andersen partners had amounted to nearly $1 billion over the years.[8] Andersen Consulting partners resented sharing their profits with Arthur Andersen and said so.

Even with the revenue-sharing contribution of Andersen Consulting, Arthur Andersen was placed in a difficult financial situation. The audit environment had not changed much from the time that the firm had first decided to grow its consulting division back in the 1970s. The threat of litigation had continued to increase during the 1980s, whereas audit revenue growth had remained disappointing compared to consulting. Before the separation, the whole partnership had shared earnings across all offices. Now the accounting partners would have a limited portion of the profits, and this had a serious effect on each accounting partner's earnings. Arthur Andersen would have to go the extra mile to bring in new business to replace the revenue they had grown accustomed to.

By 1989, Arthur Andersen contemplated building a new consulting division that would position it to recapture lost revenue and reestablish growth. But consulting in combination with audit was still perceived as a conflict of interest by the SEC, and Arthur Levitt, head of the SEC under the Clinton administration, was determined to eliminate this conflict from the public accounting profession while he was in office.

Would Arthur Andersen become a consulting firm again or return to its accounting foundations? Could it be both?

Although the firm had confronted a multitude of internal problems by hosting consulting services within its organization, the partners had not encountered any inherent external conflict of interests associated with Andersen's consulting division. Increased revenues were worth the risk, and the partners thought they could manage consulting services better the next time. This time, the Arthur Andersen partners would take a different approach, keeping consulting under the watchful eye of accounting.

Arthur Andersen decided to try consulting again. What Arthur Andersen did not recognize, as the firm moved to reestablish consulting, were the changes that had occurred within Andersen's own accounting culture as a result of its long association with the consulting division. When Arthur Andersen had enabled the consulting division to develop an aggressive entrepreneurial culture built on distinct recruitment, professional development, and career paths, it had made compromises in its own recruitment, professional development, and career path. In the process, Arthur Andersen had shifted its values in subtle and not-so-subtle ways.

The most significant shift was in Arthur Andersen's values that placed a new importance on client service. Client service was important to consulting and it topped their list of values. Arthur Andersen had learned from the best—Andersen Consulting. Influenced by Andersen Consulting's values and culture, client service had become more important to accounting. It also topped Arthur Andersen's values. While Andersen Consulting and Arthur Andersen shared the value of client service, the meaning of this value had been interpreted differently. Traditionally, client service for auditors was about ensuring compliance with regulatory requirements. For consultants, client services were about meeting client needs and satisfying the client.

Now Andersen Consulting's interpretation of client service was becoming predominant. As Arthur Andersen moved to reestablish consulting, it would learn too late that pleasing the client *was not* compatible with a public accounting firm's central responsibility to protect the public interest. But Arthur Andersen's partners had shared in the profits that a successful consulting practice could bring in, and they chose to adopt a more aggressive business model that put stress on client service and sales over stewardship. Instead of avoiding conflicts of interest, the Arthur Andersen partnership shifted its culture and values to align with those of Andersen Consulting and, in the process, came face to face with its own version of conflict of interest—a conflict between client sales and protecting the public.

References

1. Arthur Andersen & Co. 1974. *The First Sixty Years: 1913–1973*. p. 64.

2. Arthur Andersen & Co. 1974. *The First Sixty Years: 1913–1973*. p. 64.

3. Arthur Andersen & Co. 1988. *A Vision of Grandeur*. p. 185.

4. Deal, Terrence and Alan A. Kennedy. 1982. *Corporate Culture*. Reading, MA: Addison Wesley.

5. The Economist. 1988. "Accountant, Consult Thyself," *The Economist*, September 10. London: The Economist Newspaper Ltd., p. 176.

6. Arthur Andersen & Co. 1988. *A Vision of Grandeur*. p. 177.

7. The 1989 Annual Report of Arthur Andersen & Co., SC. 1989. August 31, p. 9.

8. Final Award in the Arbitration of Andersen Consulting Business Unit Member Firms versus Arthur Andersen Business Unit Firms, July 28, 2000.

6

SALES CULTURE

Arthur Andersen was faced with maintaining the Andersen name and brand under internal and external pressures. By the 1990s, competition among the major accounting firms was intensifying, and Arthur Andersen was losing clients because of its tough conservative auditing opinions.[1] Quality was still important at accounting firms such as Arthur Andersen, but success would now depend heavily on generating more revenues and improving profitability. With Andersen Consulting operating as a separate firm, Arthur Andersen lost a valuable resource and it found itself facing the same set of problems that it had faced in 1979. Audit revenue growth continued to remain flatter than desirable, and litigation was as powerful a threat as ever.

Once again, Andersen had few options available to raise money. Under U.S. federal regulation, public accounting firms could not be corporations because of the potential conflict of interest between serving the public trust and serving stockholders. Tied to the partnership model of organization, Arthur Andersen was limited in the ways it could raise capital. Arthur Andersen responded in the 1990s, as they had in 1979, by using profits to reestablish a business and computer systems consulting practice within Andersen—the Small Business Division, or tiny tickers, as they were nicknamed. The Small Business consulting group targeted consulting projects for small companies—projects too small for Andersen Consulting to be interested. Almost immediately, the tiny tickers began to grow.

The Goldman-Sachs Partnership

Andersen was not the only firm struggling to grow its business under a partnership model of organization in a competitive marketplace. Many of the old investment houses on Wall Street began operation as partnerships. In 1998 Goldman-Sachs was one of the last major partnerships left on Wall Street. Like Andersen, many of the partners at Goldman-Sachs were concerned that their company was not in a position to compete in Wall Street's very competitive market. To expand into a global company, they needed capital.[2] But for years, compensation was based on seniority, and the majority of the profits had gone to senior partners. Many at Goldman-Sachs felt that these senior partners received more than their fair share without reinvesting significantly in the firm. In 1990, Robert Rubin, head of Goldman-Sachs, had asked the partnership to reexamine the firm's profit-sharing arrangement to maximize capital. Rubin suggested an alternative compensation system to redistribute shares based on partner performance.[3] He thought that this formula would provide incentives to stimulate growth. The new compensation plan had unexpected consequences. Although the partners at Goldman-Sachs did shift their behavior to take advantage of the new opportunities opening up for high performers, they also became more interested in short-term profit through trading opportunities and lost sight of the firm's responsibilities for stewardship. In 1999, Goldman-Sachs opted to restructure as a corporation, offering stock to raise money. When the firm reorganized as a public company and issued stock, each Goldman-Sachs senior partner received an equity payment of

$125–150 million, and junior partners received $50–60 million. Goldman-Sachs' partners were accused of greed as they became more willing to take "as much risk as [they could], and make [money] as fast as [they could]."[4]

The Partner Purge of 1992

During the 1988 restructure, partners had hoped that, together, Arthur Andersen and Andersen Consulting could become the "one-stop shop" for clients. But differing understandings about the primary role of partners brought the partnership into conflict. Many of Arthur Andersen's accounting partners had worked side by side with those in consulting and had been exposed to the aggressive marketing strategies that made consulting so successful. The association had compromised Arthur Andersen's core culture based on the values and behaviors found in the auditing profession, and its conservative Midwestern roots.

Worried that increased business competition was eroding profits, some partners argued that Arthur Andersen had to adopt aggressive marketing strategies, like those used by Andersen Consulting, to stay viable, and at the 1989 partner meeting, the themes were profit and sales. The rock song "Eye of the Tiger" boomed from speakers, and a live tiger was brought on stage. The new head of the U.S. audit division, Richard Measelle, declared that raising profit would "require the eyes of a tiger, eyes that seize opportunities, eyes that are focused on the kill. It's the eye of the tiger, it's the thrill of the fight."[5] Not all audit partners in the audience were comfortable with this glitzy presentation.

The increasing pressure to be profitable placed on Arthur Andersen's partners led to drastic action—the partner purge of 1992. Arthur Andersen's audit leadership sided with those partners who believed that, if Andersen was to remain profitable, partners had to focus more on sales. Richard Measelle directed every office to undergo a performance review, based on the yearly number of chargeable hours the partners supervised. It was assumed that partners should handle about 20,000 hours of work per year. If an office billed 100,000 hours and had 10 partners, that was five too many. Those considered low performers would be asked to leave or retire. Only performance-oriented partners would be retained. Measelle justified the actions, saying, "The firm and its competitors were only facing up to the fact that they were not immune to the laws of economics."[6]

Asking so many partners to leave at once was an unprecedented event. Under almost any circumstance, Andersen was a lifetime commitment for most partners. Firms like Andersen did not lightly abandon a member in trouble, and partners felt obligated to support each other. Even if the AICPA suspended a partner's license, banning him from undertaking audits, the banned partner would be reassigned, not dismissed. Dismissal under the terms of the Partnership Agreement was possible but rarely used. It took a two-thirds vote of the partnership to oust a partner. Partners were so carefully selected and so well trained that very few serious errors in promotion were made, and few were ever asked to leave. A partner would have to have exceptional circumstances to leave voluntarily.

Many of the old guard within the partnership did not believe in the new sales orientation and were not prepared to leave. They fought back. One senior partner said, "I thought their arithmetic was a rather simplistic way of looking at things, and I told them so."[7] Arthur Andersen's values had already been compromised in the 1980s. The concessions made to accommodate the consulting division and accounting's close association with consulting's aggressive marketing strategies had influenced the thinking of some auditors and local offices. The balance between stewardship and client service was tipping toward client service and, by extension, sales. The accounting partnership was on unstable ground and, even with Arthur Andersen's separation from Andersen Consulting, Arthur Andersen's partnership was so large and so widespread that the partnership's ability to self-monitor was almost impossible. With more emphasis on sales, there was the real risk that some young partner would step over the line, compromising his accounting principles to make a sale or to keep a client happy.

The new leaders driving the purge thought they were adapting to the more competitive environment in which they had to do business. They thought they were doing the right thing. But it was impossible to account for all the unintended consequences as the combined effect of the changes came together.

The purge cut deeply, removing about 10 percent of the most conservative partners with traditional values, and increasing the value put on revenue generation through sales. Many of those removed were the most experienced individuals with a deep commitment to quality or were auditors with exceptional technical skills. They were good at conducting audits but not selling them. When Andersen lost these partners, the firm lost expertise through which quality was taught and learned. Fewer senior partners would be available to teach key audit courses in the firm's professional development program. No longer would young recruits and new managers learn from the years of experience these senior partners shared formally and informally. It reduced the number of senior experienced partners available for internal oversight groups, such as the Professional Standards Group (PSG), charged with analyzing the toughest accounting questions and making the tough calls on ambiguous technical issues.

The purge also contributed to the destabilization of the delicate balance between youth and experience within the firm. Like the rest of the firm's staff, a large proportion of partners were young. Conscious of this, the firm had a policy of assigning experienced senior partners as advisors and mentors to oversee inexperienced younger partners.

With the partner purge, the role of the partners shifted to one aligned with management and sales. One partner characterized the shift as a "corporate vice president mentality" and salesman role.

Overtly, the conflict among partners was about the shift in the role of the partner from oversight to revenue generation. But the conflict was also about whether the firm would continue safeguarding the public trust or become a multidisciplinary consulting firm in which audit played an increasingly smaller role.

The partner purge of 1992, in which a number of younger, more aggressive members of the partnership displaced more staid and conservative ones, was a defining moment for Andersen. It made public a number of value and behavioral shifts that had been brewing within the firm. Although partners had always been involved with selling the firm's services, the purge clearly prioritized this role for Arthur Andersen partners. At the same time, it removed a disproportionate number of the old-style audit partners, undercutting the blunt, straight-thinking, straight-talking values on which Andersen's early reputation and success had been based.

Building a Power Base

With the partner purge of 1992, more stress was now put on the sales role of the partner, and generating work through sales became an increasingly important performance measure. Building a network of trusted colleagues was always an important component of success at Andersen. After the purge, accounting partners intensified efforts to build sales networks, modeling their activities on those of consulting. Some of the more successful partners could trace the beginnings of their networks back to the peer-to-peer relationships that they had forged during their stays at one of the firm's education centers.

The central training facility in St. Charles, as well as regional centers, brought together members of the firm from all over the world, and the bonds formed during an Andersen training were as important as the relationships found in local offices—sometimes more important. It was not uncommon for the graduates from a particular training class to remain in contact. Some would even arrange to have weekly conference calls to stay in touch, get advice, and share success strategies. Many of the relationships lasted through an Andersen career and beyond. Importantly, these cross-office bonds provided opportunities to build a network of trusted colleagues. Arthur Andersen's partner networks stretched around the world, and work was referred wherever possible. By the early 1990s, about 30% of the work in the United Kingdom and European offices was referred by partners in the U.S.

With an increasing stress on sales, partners needed staff who would help the local practice grow, and that meant staff with saleable skills and knowledge. Partners had been conscious of the need for a mix of talent and skill in balancing technical skills against administrative abilities and leadership. Now, recruiting sales talent became increasingly important. Partners used the firm's college recruitment systems to select and screen staff to grow a local workforce with skills and knowledge that would be attractive to clients and to help with marketing their services. In the early 1980s, partners were talking about the need to find and groom a few sales staff—sometimes called "pretty boys"—to sell, but they placed a value on those who could actually deliver the services. Over time, the balance between accounting and sales skills changed in favor of more "pretty boys," and recruiting and promotion considered a candidate's sales potential, as well as accounting ability.

Partners also began to use the apprenticeship relationship to build a power base for attracting and shaping protégés. In the mentor role, the local office partners made sure that everyone shared the same goals and spoke the same language. Increasingly, that language included talk about sales and profit. In this way, partners were able to mold recruits to patterns of behavior that would support local office success. Such saleable staff became the trading cards on which partners could improve their sales positions in their networks of relationships. Again, following consulting's lead, Arthur Andersen became a complex web of local office links and partner deals, based on the need to match available staff with available work.

Generating revenue through sales or, indirectly, by lending saleable staff increasingly became the measure of success at the partner level. A partner with a growing revenue stream would climb the partner hierarchy, and his compensation would rise accordingly. In the 1990s, some partners' annual compensation went into the low seven figures, although this may seem modest in comparison with executive compensation outside the firm.

It is doubtful that Arthur Andersen's auditors would have intentionally violated their ethics but, with the shift in the role of the partner and the increasing rewards for aggressive sales, objectivity might have been more easily clouded by the possibilities of client revenues, and maintaining sales and profitability might have become more important than straight thinking and straight talking. If a high-performing partner was a little uncontrollable, it was now an acceptable risk to take in exchange for the sales ability he or she brought to the firm. Partners could not easily be prevented from making independent, although risky, decisions if their offices were profitable.

Building External Power—Building Client Relationships

There were ever-increasing stakes and pressures to generate revenue and improve profits. A diminishing proportion of the partners felt obligated to protect the public interest, and more placed emphasis on managing client relationships and promoting Andersen's many and varied services. Internally, a partner could be successful if he or she could build a partner network for trade. Externally, a partner could be successful if he or she built a network of client relationships that sold the work. The shift in Arthur Andersen's new stress on sales was reflected in the client networks that some partners were building.

Partner-client politics took on a new dimension as many of the firm's partners intensified their sales roles. When Andersen opened its doors for business, partners had understood their roles to be stewards of the public trust. Most CEOs and CFOs at the time held similar beliefs that they were the stewards of their companies—the captains of the ships of industry. This allowed accounting firms such as Andersen to align and partner with CEOs, top executives, and boards of directors in this common goal of stewardship. Both were concerned with long-term success and were there for the long haul. Values were in alignment, and close client-partner relationships had begun positively. As business became a short-term venture in the 1990s, the long-term viability of a company was not as important as demonstrating increases in quarterly profits, and CEOs and CFOs were willing to juggle the books to show those increases. In this new business environment, the goals of auditors and company executives were not aligned, and close partner-client relationships became a problem. Getting too close to clients was a trend throughout the public accounting industry, but getting close meant sales.

Partners were taught sales techniques and followed trends in improving salesmanship. The rising pressures to increase sales pushed some partners beyond their limits and discouraged many others. One partner commented on the sales pressure, saying that it encouraged achievement in the beginning but, when an individual had done as much as possible, there came a point when it was hard to do any more, and it became discouraging in the end.[8]

One cost of the sales trend was the increasing sacrifice of personal freedom required of partners. Although social responsibility through community involvement had always been encouraged at Andersen, such involvement became a means to an end as partners used community connections to court prospective clients. Sales-oriented partners became involved in their local communities and with local business leaders—professionally and socially. The spouse and family of firm members often became involved in supporting and enhancing the client relationship, becoming part of the partner-client relationship, with all family members becoming involved in some way with the firm. The daughter of an Arthur Andersen partner was once overheard to complain that there were more Andersen clients at her sister's wedding than relatives and friends.

Sometimes, former Andersen employees even became the client. It was not uncommon for Andersen people who left the firm to be placed in a client organization. Andersen had about 15% employee turnover every year between those who left voluntarily and those out-placed. Some companies even had a strong hiring preference for ex-Andersen people. They were usually competent and well trained. This type of employee "out placement" was encouraged. The firm was very conscious of the fact that former employees could make influential decisions in the firm's favor. In fact, some partners counted on it and wanted staff to leave on good terms as much as possible, because they would often be in positions in their new employment situation to influence decisions or hire the firm.

One early lesson at Core Skills, Arthur Andersen's basic management training, was that people who left the firm might become prospective clients and client team members on engagements. The people in the room today are your peers but they are tomorrow's CEOs and CFOs, recruits were told. The degree to which Andersen alumni kept in touch was unusual, compared with other companies. Jonathan Goldsmith, a former Andersen mergers-and-acquisitions consultant in Chicago, said, "I've worked for other firms where they didn't have any sort of alumni network because it was just a job. But from the first day I joined Andersen, it was like being part of a family. It's all top-notch people who are all motivated and want to be successful. Being around people like that is something that's hard to let go of."[9]

Staff at Arthur Andersen's Houston Office

As the Enron story began to break, several news organizations pointed out that members of the Arthur Andersen audit team may have gotten too close to their Enron client. The fact of the matter was that many of the Enron and Andersen employees had known and, in some cases, worked with each other for years. Arthur Andersen's audit partner, David Duncan, must have found many familiar faces among the employees working at Enron. In 1997, the year

Duncan became lead partner on the Enron engagement, his friend and ex-Andersen accountant, Richard Causey, was appointed Enron's Chief Accounting Officer. Causey is said to have favored Arthur Andersen employees and was responsible for recruiting many of them to work at Enron. Andersen alumni were a known quantity, sharing the firm's training, methodologies, and quality assurance background. Other Andersen alumni included Enron's Vice President and whistle blower, Sherron Watkins. She had started work at Arthur Andersen's Houston office in 1982, the year after David Duncan joined the firm, and worked there as an auditor until 1989. She left the Houston office to join Metallgesellschaft, where she worked with another Andersen alumni from the Houston office, Jeff McMahon. When Metallgesellschaft folded in 1993, both Jeff and Sherron went to work for Enron. At Enron, Sherron worked on "off-the-balance-sheet" SPEs, and Jeff McMahon worked first as an accountant, then as Enron's treasurer. In May 2000, McMahon directly challenged Andrew Fastow, Enron's CFO, on the financial practices he engaged in and was replaced as treasurer by Ben Glisan, yet another Andersen alumni.

In the case of auditing professionals, going to a client company was a delicate matter. There were restrictions on auditors that prevented them from going to work for a client for which they had acted as auditor. And, of course, ex-Arthurs knew all of Arthur Andersen's auditing methods and might be in a position to manipulate the firm's processes. But, with the increasing importance of profitability, alumni could be key to making a sale. Like alumni from universities, there was a special bond, including the ability to speak the same special language and a sense of obligation to help each other. Some offices even hosted regular get-togethers and alumni dinners that brought current and former firm employees together. To take full advantage of alumni, a smart partner had to make sure that staff had a good experience while in the local office. This meant providing a positive mentor experience. And, when individuals might discover they were "out" and not "up" or were being laid off during a bad economic period, many local offices learned to handle the terminations with skill to ensure continued loyalty. The partner networks established at Andersen were transformed into partner-client networks. This was good for sales.

The new stress on sales worked. Between 1988 and 1999, Andersen Worldwide's revenue jumped from just under $3 billion in 1988 to over $16 billion, and the firm more than quadrupled the number of its employees. Andersen Consulting partners, however, saw Arthur Andersen's aggressive consulting sales effort as a direct threat to their business.

The Second Consulting Revolution

The creation of the tiny tickers had reestablished consulting services within Arthur Andersen and was seen as a competitive threat by Andersen Consulting. Under Thomas Ketteman, an audit partner, Arthur Andersen actively pursued building up this new line of consulting business at Arthur Andersen. Tensions escalated between Arthur Andersen and Andersen Consulting as they bickered over clients.

In January 1990, Larry Weinbach convened the first of several Executive Committee meetings intended to resolve the competition issues between the two firms. The meeting resulted in an agreement among the partners known as the *Florida Accords*. In the Florida Accords, Arthur Andersen agreed to provide consulting services only to smaller businesses with revenue under $175 million.[10] In return, Andersen Consulting agreed to provide "strategic services, systems integration, IT consulting and change management services"[11] to large businesses over $175 million in revenue.

It was not long before their clients overlapped, and Arthur Andersen and Andersen Consulting found themselves in direct competition again. Andersen Consulting complained, and there were numerous turf wars over clients—about who could do business with whom, which clients were off limits to Andersen Consulting, and which were off limits to Arthur Andersen. The Florida Accords was followed by a number of other attempts by Weinbach to overcome the dysfunctionality and dissension[12] throughout the 1990s. But nothing seemed to solve the problem, particularly in business systems consulting, strategic services, and operational consulting.[13]

Finally, in 1997, Arthur Andersen and Andersen Consulting filed suits against each other with the International Court of Arbitration. In its suit, Andersen Consulting asked for a $400 million settlement from Arthur Andersen for violating the agreement to consult only with small businesses, for poaching staff, and for using Andersen Consulting's reputation. Arthur Andersen countered with its own suit.[14] The court appointed an arbitrator whose determination would be binding on both firms. Andersen was described in a *Wall Street Journal* article as having "a culture clash with a twist."[15] Shaheen, Andersen Consulting's head, gave a statement saying, "Not everybody sees eye to eye. We're trying desperately to sort that out." Frustrated by years of futile attempts to reconcile the two business units, Weinbach, the head of Andersen Worldwide, resigned the same year, 1997.

By 1998, the revenue transfer payment Andersen Consulting made to Arthur Andersen had reached $232 million that year,[16] and the final battle between the two divisions erupted at the annual partner meeting. With Weinbach's departure, there was a crisis in leadership. Arthur Andersen and Andersen Consulting both offered a slate of candidates along with plans for the firm's future. On the Arthur Andersen side, James Wadia offered to address the firm's problems through adjustments in the profit sharing. But at the same time, he championed open competition between the business units. Naturally, this did not go over well with Andersen Consulting. George Shaheen, Andersen Consulting's head, proposed making Andersen's worldwide organization a broad-based consulting firm with Arthur Andersen services coming under that umbrella. Naturally, this did not go over well with Arthur Andersen. Neither plan satisfied the partnership. Balloting in May 1997 and again in June failed to elect any candidates with the necessary two-thirds majority.[17] For the first time, the firm's partners were unable to agree on a single candidate for leadership of Andersen Worldwide.

Arguments at a board of partners meeting between Andersen's accounting and consulting partners became so bitter that they never got to the big dinner that had been planned. The *New York Times* ran an article the next day on "How the Andersens Turned into the Bickersons."[18] It would be the firm's last effort to hold a meeting jointly with all members of the board of partners. The firm's reputation was in tatters as the public media wrote, "Can't they figure this out? Isn't that what they are paid to do?"[19] Andersen's public relations experts were kept busy with damage control as partner relations deteriorated.

Meanwhile, the partners' stalemate over who should replace Weinbach created a leadership void at Andersen Worldwide and, in May 1997, Robert Grafton was asked to take the position on an interim basis. He remained in that office until January, 2001.

One of the reasons it took so long for Arthur Andersen and Andersen Consulting to break apart was the expense involved. To make sure that Andersen's partners stayed within the firm, a tough clause had been inserted in the partnership agreements after 1977. Leaving carried a heavy penalty of one and a half times an individual's annual revenue. Even though it was a separate firm, Andersen Consulting remained under this agreement.[20] It was a way, a consulting spokesperson said later, of keeping them shackled to the firm.

If Andersen Consulting wanted to leave as a group, the penalty to sever its ties with Arthur Andersen carried a big financial burden, too. The partnership agreement called for consulting partners to pay Arthur Andersen partners 150% of Andersen Consulting's revenue collected in the previous year. If consulting partners were going to leave Andersen, they would jointly have to take on an enormous financial burden to do so. In the lawsuits that led to the firm's dissolution, Arthur Andersen put this amount at $14.6 billion.

Because the parties could not agree on terms, the matter would have to be decided by arbitration, a process to which both sides had agreed in 1988. The "divorce" agreement between the partnerships was arbitrated by a Harvard-educated law professor in Bogotá, Columbia who was engaged to work out the details of the split. For Andersen Consulting to walk away from Arthur Andersen, its managing partner, Wadia, set the price at $150 million per year in royalties for use of Arthur Andersen technology to be paid by Andersen Consulting in perpetuity. If Andersen Consulting didn't like this arrangement, it could make a one-time pay-ment of $14.6 billion. Andersen Consulting did not really like either of these alternatives. For the next two and a half years, Arthur Andersen and Andersen Consulting were involved in legal maneuvering.

Although billions of dollars were at stake, an important sticking point in the arbitration agreement was identity. The Andersen name was in contention, in part because Andersen Consulting had just final-ized conversion to an expensive new logo. In the end, Arthur Andersen was given the name but was denied the $14.6 billion it had anticipated in exit fees. Andersen Consulting was ordered to drop Andersen as part of its identity and pay the $1 billion in revenue transfer payments and damages that had accrued between 1997 and 2000.

The two very loosely united elements of the firm officially dis-solved their connections in August 2000. Arthur Andersen announced to the world that, henceforth, it would be known "simply as Andersen." Andersen Consulting took the name Accenture and was free to do something its partners had wanted to do for a long time—go public. Accenture had its initial public offering practically before the ink was dry on the "divorce" decree.

Arthur Andersen did not anticipate that it would lose at arbitration, and once settlement was reached, the audit leadership resigned. Arthur Andersen took six months to find a new leader before it finally elected Joseph Bernardino. Bernardino was head of Arthur Andersen for only five months when Enron, then WorldCom, Qwest Communications, and Global Crossing blew up.

Shifting Values

Andersen's shift from a public accounting firm to a multiservice organization took almost 90 years. Over that time, you can look back and see how each decision the partnership made moved it away from its core business.

In Andersen's 1999 Annual Report, the core values of the firm were stated as:

1. Integrity

2. Respect

3. Passion for Excellence

4. One Firm

5. Stewardship

6. Personal Growth

The values were much closer to those of Andersen Consulting. Client Service was included in the value, Passion for Excellence.[21]

In a highly competitive business environment, Arthur Andersen's association with consulting's more aggressive sales-oriented culture deeply influenced its accounting culture and pushed accountants to adopt many of consulting's values and strategies. The partner purge of 1992 completed Arthur Andersen's transformation into a full-fledged sales culture, even though more conservative accountants fought hard to retain the old system to avoid placing Andersen's culture and values at risk.

The shift to sales was by no means wholesale. Arthur Andersen's local offices had always been independent, and many of them now chose to remain committed to the traditional values and work practices that had made the firm famous. But that commitment cost money, and it was not as easy as it had been in Arthur E. Andersen's day to walk away from a client who was willing to pay high fees for nonaudit services. With the split between Arthur Andersen and Andersen Consulting, Arthur Andersen lost an important revenue source. With finances tightening, getting and keeping lucrative client engagements became crucial. Conflicts of interest were inevitable under these circumstances, and mistakes in judgment would be made.

References

1. Strahler, Steven R. 2002. "Auditing as an Afterthought." *Crain's Chicago Business*, October 7.

2. Endlich, Lisa. 2000. *Goldman-Sachs: The Culture of Success*. London: Warner Books; Little, Brown and Company. 167–170.

3. Endlich, Lisa. 2000. *Goldman -Sachs: The Culture of Success*. London: Warner Books; Little, Brown and Company. 167–170.

4. Endlich, Lisa. 2000. *Goldman-Sachs: The Culture of Success*. London: Warner Books; Little, Brown and Company. 167–170

5. McRoberts, Flynn. 2002. "A Revolution Sweeps Andersen, Pitting Auditors Against Consultants in a Race for Higher Profit," *Chicago Tribune*, September 2.

6. McRoberts, Flynn. 2002. "A Revolution Sweeps Andersen, Pitting Auditors Against Consultants in a Race for Higher Profit," *Chicago Tribune*, September 2.

7. McRoberts, Flynn. 2002. "A Revolution Sweeps Andersen, Pitting Auditors Against Consultants in a Race for Higher Profit," *Chicago Tribune*, September 2.

8. Covaleski, Mark A. 1997. "Units Split on New Leadership." *New York Times*, June 28.

9. Fowler, Tom. 2002. "Paperwork and Regret: Employees Still at Andersen Closing Offices." *Houston Chronicle*, July 3.

10. Andersen Arbitration Documents. 1999. p. 13.

11. Andersen Arbitration Documents. 1999. p. 14.

12. Berton, Lee. 1996. "Management Andersen Flap Could Presage Formal Split," *The Wall Street Journal*, July 29.

13. Andersen Arbitration Documents. 1999. p. 21.

14. Wild, Damian. 1999. "Andersen Petitions for a Divorce." *The Independent*, October 24.

15. White, Joseph B. and Elizabeth MacDonald. 1997. "At Andersen, the Accountants Face an Unlikely Adversary: The Consulting Operation They Created Becomes Rival for Power, Prestige," *The Wall Street Journal*.

16. Crockett, Robert O. 1999. "Next Stop, Splitsville." *Business Week*, January 18.

17. Bryant, Adam. 1997. "The Andersen Family Feud; Two Units Split on New Leadership." *The New York Times*, June 28.

18. Petersen, Melody. 1998. "How the Andersens Turned into the Bickersons," *The New York Times*, March 15, Section 3, pp. 1, 13.

19. Petersen, Melody. 1998. "How the Andersens Turned into the Bickersons," *The New York Times*, March 15, Section 3, p. 1.

20. Whitford, David. 1997. "Arthur, Arthur... The Combination of Arthur Andersen and Andersen Consulting is a Consulting Services Giant. So Why Can't the Two Sides Get Along?" *Fortune*, November 10.

21. Andersen Worldwide, SC. 1999. Annual Report, September, 1999.

7

MISTAKES
IN JUDGMENT

When Arthur Andersen adopted a sales culture, the shift unbalanced many of Andersen's traditional values and practices, increased the level of risk Andersen was willing to take with its clients, and raised the possibility for conflicts of interest. After the partner purge of 1992, Arthur Andersen became involved in a number of litigations that included Sunbeam Corporation, Baptist Foundation of Arizona (BFA), Waste Management, Inc., Boston Market Trustee Corp., Department 66, and Colonial Realty. Most of these cases were settled with little media attention. The general opinion among Arthur Andersen staff was that the vast majority of auditors were trying to do the right thing but there were a few bad apples. It can also be argued that Andersen's increasing emphasis on getting and keeping clients may have clouded the judgment and pressured partners to accommodate clients.

External business pressures also played a part. Through the 1990s, the accounting profession came under increasing pressure to move from historical transaction reporting to forecasting and other emerging accounting manipulations. Organizations were even hiring PhDs in mathematics to create complex financial models that could take advantage of largely unregulated derivatives and SPEs. In the process, these companies created financial structures that few could understand. Disturbed by these trends, one accounting professor reminded everyone of a 1970s joke characterizing these practices as Cleverly Rigged Accounting Ploys (CRAP), rather than Generally Accepted Accounting Principles (GAAP).[1]

Conflicts of Interest and the SEC

The SEC has always kept an eye on the consulting activities of all of the large public accounting firms, believing that offering such services compromises auditor independence and can bias audits. Because Andersen had one of the largest consulting business units of any of the big public accounting firms, the SEC had paid particularly close attention to Arthur Andersen over the years. Auditors are required to be independent—have no ties to clients—so they can issue objective opinions on the state of client accounting. If the same firms providing audit services also receive significant fees for consulting, can they be truly independent? If consulting services were allowed, they should be limited, the SEC thought, to audit-related issues.

As early as the 1970s, Arthur Andersen's chief executive, Harvey Kapnick, had clashed with the SEC over the role of consulting services in possible conflicts of interest at Andersen. At the time, Kapnick scoffed at the idea that there could be such a conflict, suggesting that there were bigger problems than consulting besetting public accounting. He thought the SEC should pay more attention to the financial transactions in which businesses of the time were engaging. From his point of view, accounting needed to keep pace with the business practices rapidly evolving in the national and international economies of his day, and that it was business that needed better regulation so that accountants could play their part effectively. Still, Kapnick expected the SEC to crack down on Andersen's consulting division in the 1970s. The crackdown never happened, although the SEC continued to pay close attention to the firm.

In the 1990s, the single most contentious issue between the large public accounting firms and the SEC remained the threat of conflicts of interest that nonaudit services posed to the public interest. Arthur J. Levitt, Jr., Chairman of the SEC under the Clinton administration, attempted to separate audit and consulting services. He was particularly concerned that the dramatic increase in consulting revenues collected by the Big Five public accounting firms would compromise the independence of audits.

Levitt proposed restricting the amount of nonaudit consulting work that public accounting firms could do for their audit clients. Many of the large public accounting firms were opposed to any rule that denied them the ability to consult. The proposed SEC rule changes would also have banned firms from designing an audit client's compensation systems, acting as an advocate for clients by giving legal advice, or lobbying on their behalf. In addition, firms could not provide bookkeeping services, conduct appraisals of assets, recruit or evaluate client employees, or give investment advice to audit clients. Enacting such rules would have reduced the pool of audit clients available to public accounting firms if they pursued consulting engagements with those clients. The figures made public in 2000 showed the extent of accounting's ties to consulting. The Standard & Poor 500 companies reported paying $3.7 billion in nonaudit fees to their auditing firms while paying only $1.2 billion in audit fees. In one example, Sprint Corp. paid Ernst & Young $64 million for consulting and other services, and only $2.5 million for its audit. Levitt commented, "I have to wonder if any individual auditor, working on a $2.5 million audit contract, would have the guts to stand up to a CFO and question a dubious number in the books, thus possibly jeopardizing $64 million in business for the firm's consultants."[2] At the time, a managing director at Andersen said that the rule, if it passed, would cut the firm's market potential by 40 percent.

Arthur Andersen, KPMG, and Deloitte & Touche joined together to try to suppress the SEC's proposed changes, arguing that consulting helped auditors to understand the finances of contemporary organizations and was a way to assess the true value of a business entity. Under pressure from these big accounting firms, including threats from congressmen to cut SEC funding if it pressed for reforms, the SEC modified its version of the rule to one that better favored the accounting industry. The new independence rules were adopted on November 15, 2000. The new rules did require that public corporations disclose the nonaudit fees paid to their auditors but no restrictions were set on the fees that could be earned through nonaudit services. Instead, the Big Five were required to make public the amount of consulting fees they received.

The head of the SEC called the brawl with the accounting industry over this decision the most incredible fight in which he had ever been involved. Levitt described the massive public relations and lobbying efforts by the big accounting firms to stop his reform efforts as "a total war."[3] "This is a cultural change we are talking about,"[4] he said. Paul Volcker supported Levitt and said, "consulting was polluting the credibility of audit work."[5]

The SEC's new rules did nothing to deter public accounting firms from offering consulting services. In 2001, the University of Illinois conducted a study of 563 companies that used outside auditors.[6] They found that, for every $1 companies were spending on audit fees, they spent $2.69 for nonaudit services. For example, Puget Energy in Washington paid PricewaterhouseCoopers $534,000 in audit fees and $17 million for nonaudit consulting. Marriott International paid Andersen $1 million for its audit and $30 million for consulting.

In the 1990s, the consulting issue became more important at Andersen as fees rose. In 1994, Arthur Andersen collided with one of public accounting's self-monitoring groups, the Financial Accounting Standards Board (FASB). This time, the issue was about whether to recognize stock options as an expense in financial reporting. With support from Arthur Levitt, FASB wanted to ensure that stock options—a form of compensation for executives now favored in many companies, especially the startup technology companies—were placed on the record as expenses. If implemented, this practice would have reduced corporate earnings—not something any company wanted to show investors. Andersen Consulting was building a new client base among the high-tech companies of Silicon Valley, and the FASB decision on expensing stock options would not benefit Andersen Consulting's new clients or any of the high-tech industries in California. Andersen initially supported the position of the SEC and FASB. But then, Andersen, along with other big public accounting firms, came out against the FASB position. Both the SEC and the FASB considered Andersen's decision to go against expensing stock options as evidence of conflict of interest. In the opinion of the two oversight groups, Andersen was leaning too far in the direction of client interests precisely because of the success of nonaudit consulting services, and the independence of their accountants would be compromised. When the FASB came under extreme pressure for its position, Levitt asked it to back down. Levitt considers his recommendation to back down on this issue to have been his greatest mistake while head of the SEC.[7]

Although the SEC continued to monitor Arthur Andersen during the 1990s, it was limited in the actions it could take. The SEC is the federal agency that oversees and regulates public corporation financial reporting and disclosures, use of accounting principles, auditing practices, and trading activities. Because the accounting profession has been self-regulated for over a century, the SEC relied on the accounting profession's self-regulatory groups, such as the AICPA, the FASB, the Committee on Auditing Procedure, the Public Oversight Board (POB), and the Auditing Standards Board (ASB). The only part of the accounting profession that is regulated by the SEC is the attest function—the certification of public company financial statements. The bulk of rule making and standard setting is left to the accounting profession. This arrangement was implemented to avoid government red tape when the

SEC was established. Public auditing firms must register with the SEC and are bound by its rules. One of the rules to ensure auditor independence from investor interests prohibits public accounting firms from being publicly held corporations. Auditors are expected to report to the investing public "without fear or favor." Given its limited powers, the SEC watched and waited. After the Arthur Andersen partner purge of 1992, the SEC found that it was monitoring less and investigating more as the number of SEC actions against the firm and other big firms increased.

Baptist Foundation of Arizona

In the mid-1990s, the BFA was an Arthur Andersen client that engaged in illegal financial activities. The BFA was a custodian for tax-deferred individual retirement accounts. It marketed securities as a retirement vehicle for investors with the promise that certain profits would be paid to charity. In fact, BFA is alleged to have actually been running a vast Ponzi scheme in which money from new investors was used to pay off earlier investors until the whole scheme collapsed, and 13,000 elderly investors lost $590 million. At the time BFA filed for bankruptcy in November 1999, it had $650 million in total liability and listed assets of only about $290 million. Andersen's auditors claimed they were unaware of the illegal practices used by the BFA. However, in March 2001, Arthur Andersen settled out of court, paid a hefty fine, and made good on the losses by agreeing to pay $217 million in damages to investors. As part of the settlement, two Andersen partners lost their rights to practice in Arizona, and members of the Arizona Board of Accountancy began monitoring audits of Arizona companies conducted by Andersen's Phoenix office. Andersen also paid for the cost of the investigation—$640,000—to the Arizona Board of Accountancy. The firm never admitted or denied any wrongdoing in the BFA case.

Honest Accounting

During the same time period that the SEC was investigating Arthur Andersen's role in the BFA case, other Andersen offices were quietly trying to adhere to Arthur E. Andersen's example and walk away from clients who made unreasonable or unethical demands. One case involved an Arthur Andersen office in the Midwest. For over 30 years, this office had provided accounting and consulting services to a very successful multinational company and had received millions of dollars in fees for the work. It was one of the largest clients this local office served. When the client company became involved in a lawsuit, it expected Arthur Andersen's local office partner to testify in its defense. Defending a client is appropriate when explanation is important to clarify accounting issues, but giving incorrect information to help a client win a suit is unethical and illegal. In this case, the client company expected the local office partner to give misleading information. The partner declined. The client demanded Andersen testify or else. Again, the partner refused, and by standing his ground, the office lost its biggest audit client. Arthur Andersen supported the local office partner. Local offices had the autonomy to make these kinds of honest accounting decisions, and many did. The decision to walk away from this client was done quietly so that the client would not suffer any serious consequences that might result from losing its external audit firm.

Sunbeam Corporation

Some time before the Enron trial, Arthur Andersen was also implicated in improper accounting for another company—Sunbeam Corp. In this case, the SEC was concerned about the quality of Sunbeam management and its financial reporting. In 1998, Sunbeam restated earnings to correct for accounting abuses and went bankrupt under the leadership of Al Dunlap. Dunlap, known as "Chainsaw Al," was a highly visible celebrity CEO, and the case received a lot of media attention. Dunlap was hired by Sunbeam because of his reputation as a "turnaround specialist." According to the SEC's charges, Dunlap and others engaged in fraudulent accounting to create the illusion of a successful restructuring at Sunbeam. Included in the complaint were allegations that the company recorded revenue on contingent sales, accelerated sales from later periods into the present quarter, and used improper bill-and-hold transactions to make the company look more profitable.

With the restatement of Sunbeam's earnings for 1997 and 1998, Sunbeam's net income dropped from $109.4 million to $38.3 million. Sunbeam's stockholders decided to file a civil suit against several Sunbeam executives, as well as an Andersen partner, over mismanagement of funds, and the case came to the SEC's attention. Andersen tried to prevent the restatements from being introduced as evidence, but they were used and Sunbeam's executives were eventually indicted. Deloitte & Touche was called in to help Andersen review the Sunbeam accounts. It was eventually decided that Dunlap had overstated Sunbeam's losses in 1996, the year prior to his takeover. He then overstated gains in 1997 and 1998 giving the appearance of a quick turnaround that boosted the stock price. In the opinion of the SEC, the lead auditor at Sunbeam should not have signed off on Sunbeam's financials. Andersen maintained that the partner had acted with the appropriate degree of skepticism and exercised professional judgment. The SEC characterized this as an instance of massive financial fraud. Sunbeam filed for Chapter 11 bankruptcy in February 2001, and in April 2001, Andersen settled the case out of court, agreeing to a $110 million payment to Sunbeam shareholders. Arthur Andersen did so without admitting or denying guilt.

Waste Management, Inc.

For 30 years, Waste Management, Inc., a large trash disposal company, had retained Arthur Andersen as its auditor. Between 1992 and 1996, Waste Management overstated pretax income by $1 billion while hid-ing $1.7 billion in expenses[8] with Arthur Andersen's signoff. When Waste Management restated its income in 1998, the SEC began an investigation.

In June of that year, the SEC found that Andersen's audit reports were materially false and misleading for the years between 1992 and 1996 and that the firm engaged in improper professional conduct. It was the opinion of the SEC that Arthur Andersen's auditors had betrayed their allegiance to the shareholders and the public interest by failing to stand up to company management. Andersen defended its auditors by claiming that the allowed expenses were appropriate and that Arthur Andersen auditors had proposed a series of action steps to bring Waste Management's future accounting practices into line with GAAP. In the end, Arthur Andersen paid an SEC fine of $7 million to settle out of court. At the time, this was the largest fine levied against an accounting firm. One of the Arthur Andersen partners involved with Waste Management paid a civil penalty of $50,000 and lost his CPA license for five years. Two other partners paid civil penalties of $40,000 and $30,000 and lost their licenses for three years. A fourth partner lost his license for a year. Ironically, one of these partners was later appointed to head Arthur Andersen Worldwide's Risk Management Group, the body responsible for formulating Arthur Andersen's document retention policy. Once again, in this case, Arthur Andersen settled without admitting or denying the allegations or findings but did agree to be censured under the SEC's rules of practice.

Although the SEC's settlement action with Arthur Andersen did not mention auditor independence violations, it did include a comparison of fees collected by Andersen Consulting of $11.8 million to those collected by Arthur Andersen of $7.5 million.[9] Acting SEC Chairman, Laura Unger, commented in a June 26, 1998 *Wall Street Journal* article that the SEC now had a "smoking gun"[10] illustrating a clear instance where an auditor's independence was compromised. Arthur Andersen claimed that there was no independence violation and that the SEC had no case to make such a charge.

The case did raise questions about how cozy the accounting industry was getting with its audit clients. Commenting on the Andersen settlement, one member of a professional ethics committee said that, although it was not appropriate to generalize to all of accounting from the single Andersen case, it did appear that the profession needed to be more aware of the demanding role of financial reporting and its effect on accounting clients, as well as on the investing public and readers of financial statements.

It is important in the story of Arthur Andersen's collapse to know that there were similarities between events at Sunbeam, Waste Management, and Enron. At Sunbeam, documents had been shredded that allegedly might have helped the investigation of Sunbeam's management; and at Waste Management, many top financial executives and staff were former Andersen employees. Documents under Arthur Andersen control—and required to investigate the Waste Management case—disappeared. Although the SEC did not bring a criminal charge of obstruction of justice in these cases, it did raise concerns about possible violations of the antifraud provisions of the federal securities laws at Waste Management[11] and warned Arthur Andersen that if it were ever involved in a similar case, the consequences would be more severe.

Audit Failures Among the Big Public Accounting Firms

Arthur Andersen was not the only one of the Big Five public accounting firms to be compromised. KPMG audited Xerox, which had inflated pretax earnings by $1.5 billion and had to issue a restatement of about $6.4 billion. PricewaterhouseCoopers was the accountant for Microstrategy, which had to correct three years of earnings, revealing that it was losing money and was not profitable, as the financial statements had suggested.

Ernst & Young faced allegations of fraud for covering up irregularities in the books of Superior Bank, an Illinois savings and loan. The U.S. government was seeking $2 billion in fines and punitive damages, and charged that Ernst & Young attempted to cover up the Superior Bank situation because it was completing an $11 billion deal to sell its consulting practice to Cap Gemini. In 1997, Levitt received an anonymous letter alleging that auditors in the Tampa, Florida office of Coopers & Lybrand owned stock in some of their client companies. This was a violation of the independence rules. After the SEC investigation began, Coopers & Lybrand merged with Price Waterhouse. The SEC pushed for an internal audit of stock ownership in the combined firm, PricewaterhouseCoopers. The investigation found 8,000 violations involving half the firm's partners, which was more widespread than initially thought.

Competition between the Big Five public accounting firms increased the lawsuits among them. During the recession of the early 1990s, big public accounting firms sued each other over alleged negligence in handling the accounts of clients who had failed.[12] Ernst & Young sued Touche Ross; Touche Ross sued Ernst & Young and Price Waterhouse. Price Waterhouse sued Touche Ross; KPMG sued Coopers & Lybrand.

In November 2000, Donald J. Kirk, a member of accounting's Public Oversight Board stated, "We've been through a critical phase in the last two years involving a very significant failure in self-regulation—the failure to police compliance with our own rules on independence dealing with financial interest in clients ... rooted ... in our failure to recognize how times have changed. And that, I'm afraid to say, sowed many of the seeds of the struggle that's going on right now among regulators and legislators and the profession."[13] Then, WorldCom surpassed Enron as the largest bankruptcy in U.S. history. Global Crossing, Ltd. filed for bankruptcy on January 28, 2002. Then, Qwest Communications International, Inc. revealed that it had overstated revenue between 1999 and 2001 by $1.48 billion. The auditor for all three companies was Arthur Andersen.

Risk Management

Arthur Andersen's history of suspected audit mismanagement played a role in the Justice Department's conduct of the Enron trial. The SEC accused Andersen not of accounting fraud but of obstructing its ongoing investigation of Enron's "off-the-books" business. When Assistant Attorney General Michael Chertoff, chief of the Justice Department's criminal division, was put in charge of Andersen's obstruction of justice case, he concluded that Andersen was a "recidivist" and deserved stiff punishment.[14]

Of course, Andersen did not ignore the SEC's warnings. Enron typified the new, higher-risk Andersen client that was apt to use aggressive accounting.[15] Andersen[16] and all the big public accounting firms[17] had mechanisms in place for audit oversight, quality assurance, and client risk assessment to manage their high-risk clients. Arthur Andersen's Quality Assurance Program included regular audit engagement reviews by outside Quality Assurance Partners, and they conducted routine reviews of Andersen's audit team at Enron. "This is part of the normal process we go through every year in each country around the world in which we practice," Berardino, Andersen's CEO, told NBC. "We review each of our auditing clients, their accounting practices, people we've assigned to the account, and we make a decision as to whether we retain the client or not.[18]

Arthur Andersen also had a Worldwide Risk Management Group, which conducted annual reviews to rate clients' accounting methods and internal accounting teams according to degree of risk. Enron was among 50 clients receiving the firm's "maximum risk" rating.

Arthur Andersen also used a nontraditional audit process at Enron called "integrated audit." In an integrated audit, external and internal auditors work together to assess accounting processes and internal controls. This type of audit was promoted because—in theory—it could better detect and prevent problems before they happened rather than waiting until the end of a financial period to examine a company's books. However, the SEC held a very different opinion about how integrated audit was conducted at Enron. Although not illegal, the SEC did not like the integrated audit process at Enron because Arthur Andersen held a five-year contract[19] for many internal audit functions.[20] Under this arrangement, the SEC argued, external auditors would be auditing their own internal auditing work and lose both objectivity and independence. The SEC reacted by enacting rules to restrict external auditors from performing internal audit to 40% of the work.[21] Ken Lay, Enron's CEO, defended integrated audit in a letter to Arthur Levitt, head of the SEC, objecting to the 40 percent restriction and the affects it would have on Enron's integrated audit process. In the wake of Enron's eventual fall, external auditors are now entirely prohibited from providing internal audit services.

Risk was also managed by Arthur Andersen's *Professional Standards Group* (PSG). This group of senior, experienced auditors was consulted whenever an audit involved difficult technical issues or judgment calls. People in the profession often say accounting is more art than science, and the PSG members were masters of the art. One senior audit partner explained, "You always checked." Having another set of eyes on an audit was common practice, and experienced partners routinely checked with other partners and with the PSG. Given these safeguards, many within the Andersen partnership believed that risk was under control.

Errors in Judgment at Enron

In retrospect, some Arthur Andersen partners have speculated that David Duncan was, in many respects, just too young and inexperienced to handle the responsibilities he was given on the Enron account. David Duncan, the lead partner on the Enron audit, joined Arthur Andersen in 1981 and climbed the firm hierarchy, becoming a partner in 1995. His profile matched that of an Arthur Android but he also represented the 1990s generation within the firm. Typical of most Andersen staff, his friends were Andersen or former Andersen employees. In 1997, one of Duncan's friends and former Andersen employee, Richard Causey, became the Chief Accounting Officer at Enron; that same year, David Duncan became the global engagement partner and partner in charge for the Enron engagement. Arthur Andersen often attempted to match its personnel to its client counterparts in personality, style, and even age. It was also thought that Duncan's youth and aggressiveness would fit well in Enron's "cowboy culture."[22] Enron was one of the firm's largest clients, and this was a gigantic engagement expected to be worth as much as $100 million in revenue. David Duncan, along with a large team of up to 100 Andersen staff and managers, had a whole floor available to them at Enron's headquarters.

Working at Enron was considered a difficult but career-building assignment. For many of the young Andersen employees in their 20s, working on such a high-profile engagement had the potential to enhance their budding careers and maybe catch the eye of an important partner. Staff eagerly volunteered for a spot there, and Duncan should have been able to handpick his Andersen audit team from the best of the best.

But Enron was classified as one of the firm's highest-risk clients. Duncan and his team were handling a potential time bomb.

Because of Enron's complex accounting, the PSG was consulted on many of Enron's SPE deals. PSG members, Ben Neuhausen and Carl Bass, warned David Duncan that, in their judgment, some of these Enron deals were clearly wrong. Carl Bass stated, "I do not know if he [Duncan] knows how much we cannot support this" and "I did not see any way this worked." But this advice was ignored or misrepresented. At Enron's request, Carl Bass was removed from further Enron reviews. Removal of a partner at the client's request was highly unusual. Local offices remained semi-independent and an engagement partner had the right to override the PSG's opinions, but it was a very unusual thing to do. Without telling the PSG, David Duncan apparently did ignore it. For many Arthur Andersen partners, ignoring PSG's opinion was unthinkable.[23]

Because he was a junior partner, David Duncan would have had a more senior partner assigned to the account. In Duncan's case, Michael Odom, the energy practice director in the Houston Office, played this role, and he supported Duncan's decisions to ignore the advice of the PSG and override Carl Bass. David Duncan may have been given this kind of independence to maintain Enron as a client during a financially difficult time for Arthur Andersen. The firm had just lost its consulting business, Andersen Consulting, in a bitter divorce and the firm needed to retain its client base. Because David Duncan was bringing in significant revenue from Enron, to some, he was a star. At the annual partner meeting held in New Orleans in October 2001, several thousand employees gathered at a "glitzy, high-tech affair"[24] where David Duncan was one of the faces that flashed on giant video monitors. "The future is you," a voice later thundered through the hall."[25] But Arthur Andersen's future was far different than the partners gathered at this meeting could imagine. Within months, Arthur Andersen would be indicted on obstruction of justice, and David Duncan, one of the firm's stars, would not only be dismissed from the firm but would become "a symbol of the new breed of auditor...who compromised sound accounting for the sake of profit."[26]

Indictment and Trial

Initially, Andersen tried to reach an Enron settlement with the Department of Justice[27] offering to pay fines and shareholder claims, and to radically reform the firm under the leadership of Paul Volcker, but the bankruptcy of its professional liability insurer[28] forced Andersen representatives to reduce the amount of money they could offer. Reportedly, Andersen's reading of the depth of the government's anger in the Enron case was misguided.[29] The Justice Department, having secured David Duncan's confession to obstruction of justice, filed a sealed indictment against Arthur Andersen LLP in the United States District Court in the Southern District of Texas on March 7, 2002. The indictment was publicly announced March 14, 2002.

The indictment focused on obstruction of justice. The indictment claimed that a systematic effort was undertaken and carried out to purge Enron's documents, computer hard drives, and email system. The whole

U.S. firm was indicted because the Justice Department claimed that Andersen staff in Portland, Oregon; Chicago; and London had worked on the Enron account and had destroyed Enron material, as well. The indictment also described how the Enron's earnings restatement had affected the stock price of Enron shares and its stockholders. The Department of Justice did not accuse Andersen of accounting fraud but stated that "through its partners and others, [the firm did] knowingly, intentionally, and corruptly persuade and attempt to persuade other persons" to withhold, alter, and destroy records with intent to impair their integrity and availability for use in those official proceedings.[30] Document destruction became the main focus of the trial.[31]

Andersen expected to win the obstruction of justice case,[32] believing that the Department of Justice had a "dearth of credible evidence" regarding the destruction of documents[33] and that risk was under control. The Andersen attorney expressed his sentiment that the indictment against the whole firm was an action without precedent, an extraordinary abuse of prosecutorial discretion, and an abuse of government power,[34] and that the obstruction of justice trial was going to be like a Super Bowl, with a lot of buildup followed by an anticlimax, a flop.

Many inside and outside Andersen believed the indictment was a politically expedient solution to try to restore investor confidence in the American economic system. Some also believed that those in the Justice Department simply did not fully understand the consequences of indicting the firm and that, by doing so, the firm would be put out of business. Enron investors who were hoping to recover some of their losses from the firm wrote letters to members of the government, pointing out that if the firm was put out of business, their chances of getting compensation from Andersen were greatly reduced. Prominent media figures, such as Lou Dobbs, editorialized on the Andersen matter, suggesting that an indictment of the entire firm would be unfair. All of this was moot once the indictment was filed against Arthur Andersen in March 2002.

Once the trial began, there were numerous surprises. In an unusual ruling, the judge allowed the prosecution to establish a motive for the Enron shredding by presenting Andersen's prior out-of-court settlements. This ruling made the jury aware of Andersen's involvement with Sunbeam Corporation and Waste Management, Inc., and suggested that Andersen had previously tried to cover up evidence of wrongdoing.[35] David Duncan, appearing unexpectedly as a witness for the prosecution, told the court that, after taking several months to think it over, he had decided that he had obstructed justice by ordering the shredding of Enron documents. He also maintained that there had been no accounting fraud. Some members of the jury did not believe that Duncan was a credible witness or that the shredding of documents was proof of obstruction of justice.

In his opening argument Andersen's lawyers tried to give the firm a human face, asking the jury, "Who is Arthur Andersen?" He then answered that Arthur Andersen was its employees—not some abstract organization—and called the government's action against Andersen one of the greatest tragedies in the history of the criminal justice system. He even accused the government of witness intimidation. An observer stated that this was a firm that truly believed in its innocence and was apparently willing to go to its death to prove it.[36]

References

1. Briloff, Abraham. 1976. *More Debits than Credits: The Burnt Investor's Guide to Financial Statements*, New York: HarperCollins.

2. Levitt, Arthur. 2002. *Take on the Street*, New York: Pantheon Books. p. 138.

3. Mayer, Jane. 2002. "The Accountants' War," *The New Yorker*, April 22 & 29, p. 64.

4. Norris, Floyd. 2000. "A War the Accountants Will Lose Even If They Win," *The New York Times*, July 28, p. C1.

5. McRoberts, Flynn. 2002. "Faulty Decision and Strategy in Andersen's Final Months Set the Firm up for Its Collapse," *Chicago Tribune*, September 4.

6. Byrnes, Nanette, Mike McNamee, Diane Brady, Louis Lavelle, and Christopher Palmeri. 2002. "Accounting in Crisis." Special Report: The Enron Scandal, *Business Week Online*, January 28, p. 6.

7. Levitt, Arthur Jr. 2002. *Take on the Street*, New York: Pantheon Books. p. 123.

8. Levitt, Arthur Jr. 2002. *Take on the Street*, New York: Pantheon Books. p. 123.

9. Delistings, Withdrawals and Enforcement Proceedings. Arthur Andersen LLP and Three Partners Settle Civil Injunction Suit. 2001. *SEC Digest*. Issues 2001-117 through 2001-121 for the week ending June 22.

10. *The Wall Street Journal*, 1998, June 26.

11. Delistings, Withdrawals and Enforcement Proceedings. Arthur Andersen LLP and Three Partners Settle Civil Injunctive Action. 2001. *SEC Digest*. Issues 2001-117 through 2001-121 for the week ending June 22.

12. Foot, Paul 2000. *Medes and Persians*.

13. Kirk, Donald J. 2000. Conference on Challenge and Achievement in Accounting During the Twentieth Century, Panel Discussion: The Accounting Profession in the United States, The Accounting Hall of Fame, November 9–11.

14. McRoberts, Flynn. 2002. "Repeat Offender Gets Stiff Justice," *Chicago Tribune*, September 4.

15. Associated Press. 2002. "Andersen Partner Advised against Shredding," June 15.

16. Associated Press. 2002. "Andersen Partner Advised against Shredding," June 15.

17. Nader, Ralph. *Citizenworks. www.citizenworks.org*. Accessed October 27, 2002.

18. CNN. Washington. 2002. "Andersen CEO Admits to Mistakes with Enron." January 20.

19. McRoberts, Flynn, "Ties to Enron Blinded Andersen," *Chicago Tribune*, September 3, 2002.

20. Levitt, Arthur, 2002, *Take on the Street*, New York: Pantheon Books, p. 299

21. WorldNet Daily, "Did Andersen Violate 40% Rule with Enron?, April 15, 2002. *www.worldnetdaily.com/news/article.asp?ARTICLE_ID=27267*. Accessed January 30, 2003.

22. Eavis, Peter. "Enron Reaps What Its Cowboy Culture Sowed," *www.thestreet .com/_yahoo/markets/detox/10004675.html*, November 29, 2001.

23. Interviews with former partners.

24. McRoberts, Flynn. 2002. "Ties to Enron Blinded Andersen," *Chicago Tribune*, September 3.

25. McRoberts, Flynn. 2002. "Ties to Enron Blinded Andersen," *Chicago Tribune*, September 3.

26. McRoberts, Flynn. 2002. "Ties to Enron Blinded Andersen," *Chicago Tribune*, September 3.

27. McRoberts, Flynn. 2002. "Repeat Offender Gets Stiff Justice," *Chicago Tribune*, September 4.

28. Weil, Jonathan and Devon Spurgeon. 2002. "Arthur Andersen Insurer Is Rendered Insolvent—Funds from Bermuda Firm Were Going to Be Used to Settle Host of Claims." *The Wall Street Journal*, April 1.

29. Eichenwald, Kurt. 2002. "Andersen Misread Depths of the Government's Anger." *The New York Times*, March 18.

30. *Indictment: US vs. Arthur Andersen LLP.* U.S. District Court, Southern District of Texas, March 7, 2002.

31. Flood, Mary. 2002. "Trial to Focus on the Motive for Shredding." *Houston Chronicle,* May 7.

32. Eichenwald, Kurt. 2002. "A Gamble Andersen May Regret." *The New York Times,* April 29.

33. Andersen Legal Team Response to the Indictment. *www.nysccpa.org/home/ 2002/302/week/article46.html.* Accessed March 10, 2003.

34. Lawson, Milton. 2002. "Jury Selected for Andersen Trial." *Washington Times,* May 6.

35. Eichenwald, Kurt. 2002. "Judge's Ruling on Andersen Hurts Defense." *The New York Times,* July 15.

36. The Associated Press. 2002. "Andersen Trial Gets Underway." *The Houston Chronicle,* May 15.

8

UNRAVELING

Working for Arthur Andersen was not for everyone. It could be a tough culture. It was much too hierarchical and "top down" for the more free-spirited. Many people left after less than two years, believing the rewards did not warrant the demands that were made on them. Others learned to play by the rules, and some even thrived. To remain in the firm, staff members were expected to work hard, respect the authority of rank, and maintain a high level of conformity. In return, they were rewarded with support, promotion, and the possibility of making partner. Those individuals who made a career with the firm grew old together, professionally as well as personally, and most had never worked anywhere else. To these survivors, Andersen was their second family, and they developed strong loyalties to the firm and its culture.

Despite rumors before the indictment of Arthur Andersen regarding the Enron audit engagement, staff continued to go about daily work activities of traveling to job sites, finalizing reports, or preparing client presentations. Auditors were gearing up for fourth-quarter financial statements. New staff members were on their first assignments. More senior employees were thinking about possible promotion on "Bean Day," the day people found out whether they would be promoted or asked to leave the firm. Joseph Berardino, Andersen's newly elected CEO, was in Tokyo, trying to convince his partners not to overreact to the rumors circulating in the U.S., when he got a 2 A.M. phone call on March 2, 2002 letting him know that federal prosecutors were ready to indict Arthur Andersen.

Berardino had grown up with the firm, joining Arthur Andersen in 1972 after graduating from Fairfield University, just a few months before Leonard Spacek retired.[1] He became a partner by the age of 32. The straight-talking Berardino had just been elected as CEO of Arthur Andersen in January 2001, largely because of his sales ability. "Clients like Joe," Richard Measelle, former head of Arthur Andersen, commented.[2] When he became head of the firm, Berardino was faced with the tough job of moving the firm forward after the difficult split between Arthur Andersen and Andersen Consulting. So, after his election as CEO, he went on a meet-and-greet tour of major clients that included a visit to Jeffrey Skilling and Rick Causey at Enron.

Joe Berardino was as surprised as the rest of Arthur Andersen's 85,000 employees when the indictment was made. When he learned that the firm was about to be indicted, he returned to the U.S. to meet with Andersen's governing board of partners. Board members were shocked, asking, "How could we have let this happen?"[3] He then moved to begin merger talks with Deloitte & Touche and KPMG, but it was too late. After the indictment, Arthur Andersen clients began to cancel their contracts, including Sara Lee Abbott and Brunswick Corporation. Berardino, pressured to resign, stepped down on March 26, 2002 at age 51. To the end, Berardino insisted that Enron was the result of poor business decisions, not errors, explaining, "At the end of the day, we do not cause companies to fail."[4]

What bothers Andersen people most is the loss of reputation. Andersen people had always thought of themselves as ethical. Around the world, Andersen staff marched and chanted, "We are Andersen!" and "We're not going anywhere!"[5] Yellow ribbons appeared on office windows, hung up by Andersen employees who were certain that the firm was being victimized. Partners in Paris wrote, "The Americans stood behind us, we're going to stand behind them."[6]

In hindsight, there is speculation that Berardino totally misread the situation. Some partners feel Berardino should have stood up to the Justice Department. Other former partners don't think that anything the firm did would have mattered. When it became clear that Andersen was crumbling, the response of Andersen staff shifted from anger to sadness. It was apparent that the unscrupulous actions of a few were bringing down the whole firm. How could one of their own have strayed so far from the values and standards that the majority of Andersen employees respected? Why hadn't the partners stepped in more aggressively? A few Andersen insiders worried, "Is Enron the only one we have? What will happen if others come out?" What had Andersen done wrong for such a drift in values to have occurred?

Ninety-year-old Joseph Glickauf, Jr., the man responsible for introducing IT services into the firm, was amazed at how quickly everything unraveled, "We had such careful selection of those we employed," he said. "They were trained and trained and trained. You can't put Humpty Dumpty back together again."[7]

A number of former Andersen employees were interviewed during the writing of this book. The following are a representative sample of their reactions.

Other Side of the World—An "Inside" Perspective from Asia[8]

Harry James, an Andersen employee based in the city of Singapore, was one of those mystified employees. There was only one Andersen office in Singapore, but it was not small. Well over 30 partners managed almost 1,200 people and offered all of the Andersen services provided by offices in the United States, including tax, audit, business consulting, corporate finance, risk consulting, and IT solutions.

Harry and several of his colleagues from Andersen's Singapore office had attended a regional meeting in Beijing, China and had been assured by Andersen's CEO, Joe Berardino, that everything was going to be okay.

In January 2003, Harry James describes his experience of the last year. He explained:

> I was recruited by the Asia-Pacific office when I graduated from university in England and was sent to Singapore. I joined as staff and was promoted in 2001. So I was a Senior for less than a year before the whole thing happened. I was definitely planning to stay at Andersen. In fact, it never crossed my mind to leave.
>
> Andersen was a good place to work. The culture was very much that of a family. We all held the same beliefs, the same "Think straight—Talk straight" culture. We breathed it, and we lived it. So when all this happened, it was really shocking to the majority of us. I can tell you no other word but shocked. As far as we were concerned, we were a good firm. We did the right things, and we did our best. We worked hard, and we played hard. I made many good friends in my three years there from other offices in the Asia-Pacific region because we worked so closely

together on projects. These are things you can't replace with a higher salary.

Andersen was willing to invest a lot more in the welfare of its employees, too. One great example was the training program. I can safely say there was a lot of money invested. It brought people together. I always looked forward to regional or global training because it was like getting together with old friends.

I could not say what was right and what was wrong, but the one point I want to get across is that there were a lot of good people working at Andersen. And a lot of people lost their jobs for, I would say, no reason at all. To us, it just wasn't fair. And I am talking about people all over the world. Who would have thought? We were so far away from all that was happening in the States. But it certainly filtered down to us. There was no running away from it.

His comments shifted to the day Harry learned that Arthur Andersen was in trouble.

The first sign we all had that Andersen was in trouble was when we heard about it on CNN. After that, I followed the trial every day on CNN. I think people around here were just in shock for the longest time because nobody could believe it possible that something like that could go wrong. We were so far removed from everything. We couldn't believe it could really be happening.

Of course, some of us said that it would just blow over like it always does. It wasn't the first time. This had happened at other accounting firms and had always blown over. It wasn't going to be a big deal. But a couple of my colleagues didn't think the SEC would back down. They wanted a scapegoat. One even thought it was going to cause our downfall. There were a few of us who actually thought it would affect us all the way out here. At the end of March 2002, Andersen's Asia-Pacific offices started to split up and were going their own way. My boss decided to join one of the other big four accounting firms that were left.

The Singapore office merged with Ernst & Young on July 1, 2002. We had about 1,200 people in the Singapore office. By the time we merged with Ernst & Young, there were only 500 left. So you can see, 700 people had to leave. Some were laid off. Others decided to go their own way to some of the other firms. Of course, for me it is unfair. I am not going to sit here and blame someone, because there are a lot of people I could possibly blame. It is just a sad thing.

Andersen people were very proud of our culture and so proud of who we were. We all shared the same values and had that certain pride. For me, it will never be the same as it was working for Andersen. And I dare say it is a common feeling with a lot of Andersen people.

Offices Began Slipping Away—An "Inside" Perspective from Europe[9]

As the Enron events were unfolding, concerned staff members began asking partners whether they should start looking for new jobs. Everyone knew that an obstruction-of-justice indictment, even without a conviction, would have negative repercussions. Partners tried to assure staff that if worse came to worst, they would do all they could to help, and many did. "Taking care of its own" was a core value in the partnership. At the end, it was clear that this value was still strong. From staff to manager to partner, Andersen people looked out for each other as best they could. That is how Christine Burk and John Young remembered it. Both Christine and John had been managers at Arthur Andersen offices in the United Kingdom. Christine commented:

> Well, I guess you want to know what I thought of Enron. I suppose I heard about it first in November 2001.... No, maybe October. Anyway, when I heard about it, I was worried. John Young worked in the office next to mine, and I knew he followed the business press and stayed current on business. It's not one of my strengths.
>
> So I asked him what he thought, and he said it would be all right. Andersen was such a big firm and, of course, we'd been through it before. But I was worried. There was something really wrong. I knew things weren't right because of the delays and postponements of trainings. I guess I knew for sure about Andersen's collapse in February when they started canceling courses. I watched on the news about Andersen's indictment. From March on, I watched CNN every night at 11 o'clock. I wasn't sure if I was going to have a job. What was going to happen? But the indictment was the end of it. I mean there was no doubt that was the end of it. We had to undo everything we had done. It was heartbreaking.
>
> The writing had been on the wall for some time when Andersen's Russian offices decided to go with other firms. Moscow went with another firm. It was a better deal for them. Life was gradually slipping away, and then I heard that the UK offices were looking at merging with Deloitte.

John Young had been a senior manager in Andersen's tax practice in the U.K. and is very proud of his association with Andersen and of his tax practice group. He likes to describe it as "one big family," and he misses his friends, "not because we got hammered together," he points out, "but because we worked very well together." Like many

Andersen alumni, John and Christine had kept in touch after Arthur Andersen's breakup.

> Enron, I just can't understand Enron. It was either stupid or corrupt. I cannot believe that Andersen's CEO did not know about it. There were so many warnings. I read about Waste Management and Sunbeam and Baptist Foundation, and I said we have to be more careful. At first, we thought we could ride it out. Shredding papers? I couldn't give a damn what papers they shredded. Andersen was a sacrificial lamb—sacrificed on the altar of expediency. I was very, very angry from March onwards. I watched every news bulletin on the Internet. To me, it seemed as if there was a massive attack on Andersen by the American Justice Department.
>
> It wasn't long before practices began to shear off—leave Andersen. Soon, it was a free-for-all. My group was keen to stay together. It made no sense for tax to break up for the common good. There were some great partners who were really trying to keep the practice together. One, in particular, worked hard to keep it together.

He looked disappointed as he described how some Andersen people had been able to stay together at UK Deloitte & Touche, while others had left to find work with another firm.

Christine added that she had gone with another firm. "The people there are very bright, just like Andersen, but more consultative. At Andersen, we genuinely had a sense of working for the good of a global organization. The firm I am with now doesn't have a sense of global reach."

John said, "I am not ashamed to have Andersen on my CV. I am proud of it, and I will not take it off. I am known as ex-Andersen at my new firm.

"We had a different perspective at Andersen," John explained "If you were good enough, you'd be promoted. You had a sense of going places. I went to New Manager training at St. Charles, Illinois. That training was like the firm's glue. There were all these people from Norway and France and Germany and everywhere, and I thought, this is tremendous. You know, the Americans were so passionate about Andersen [that] if they had a dog, they'd call it Arthur."

"Was it really greed? Andersen had a culture and expectations of wealth, but greed doesn't seem to have played a part," he decided, and Christine nodded in agreement.

"Those were the good old days," he said, "and the world is far too tough now. The quality of people at Andersen was the best. I am very proud of Andersen, and I am not happy going to another firm. It hurts a helluva lot."

Unraveling—An "Inside" Perspective from the Midwestern U.S.[10]

Most Andersen people, even partners, didn't know much more about the Enron debacle than the general public. Many of the auditors did not know David Duncan or much about the Enron engagements.[11] Both current and former employees were equally mystified when the indictment was made. Yellow ribbons appeared on office windows in Chicago, hung up by Andersen employees who were certain that the firm was being victimized. When it became clear that Andersen was crumbling, some in the public expressed a certain satisfaction that justice was served.

Within Andersen, the response shifted from mystification to sadness. It was apparent that the unscrupulous actions of a few were bringing down the entire firm. How could one of their own have strayed so far from the values and standards that the majority of Andersen employees respected? One retired partner confessed that he just could

not comprehend how all the firm's safeguards could have been sub-
verted at Enron, not just by Enron management, but by the firm's own
people. "I'm still amazed about how quickly everything unraveled. I
mean, a year ago there was still a firm there, and today there isn't." Jill
Myers, a former Andersen Audit Manager from the Midwestern U.S.,
sat in the kitchen of her foursquare prairie home in eastern Iowa. "Over
that time, I saw the firm change quite a lot," she explained. "When I
first joined the firm, there was a sensitivity to employees and a concern
about the family–work balance. In December 2000 or January 2001, it
seemed that the tone of the firm changed."

Andersen was becoming concerned about cost cutting. It began
moving away from the values that promoted concern for the employee.

"It felt like the firm was saying we don't have to care about you as
much, so we are not going to." Jill said. For Jill, changes in the firm
really hit home when it dropped Growth and Retention of Women
(GROW), an initiative that was particularly close to her heart. "Really,
it wasn't just about women but about everyone in the firm and making
Andersen a more friendly place, a family-friendly place."

Before joining Andersen, Jill had acquired an undergraduate
degree in business at the Loyola University. But she didn't want to go
into business, so she decided to get a master's in education. As part of
her master's program, she did an internship at the Andersen training
center in St. Charles, Illinois. When she finished her internship, she
received a job offer from the Audit Division. She started "at the bottom
rung," as was typical of most staff hired by Andersen. After about six
years with the firm, she became an audit manager. "I didn't expect to
stay for more than six months when I first went to Andersen. But
Andersen kept providing good opportunities to learn and to grow. So
there was a reason to stay." Most of her time with Andersen was at St.
Charles but she also had short-term assignments in a variety of other
places, attending meetings abroad, teaching in Asia, and even spending
six months at Andersen's London office.

Jill was in St. Charles on October 16 when Enron made the announcement that it was going to take a billion-dollar write-off. Prior to the announcement in October, most people in St. Charles didn't even know that Enron was a client. Most of the St. Charles staff didn't work directly with clients and "It [Enron] just was not on the radar screen." Jill knew that Enron was a client but had no idea what services Andersen provided to it. Andersen had been sued before over an audit and had been able to negotiate a settlement. "I'd say the attitude that summarized the reaction of people in St. Charles was no big deal. It's happened so many times before," Jill explained. "I had never heard of David Duncan. I think the St. Charles employees might have felt insulated." Even after Enron declared bankruptcy, the staff at St. Charles didn't think the Enron scandal would affect them. And anyway, what was happening at Arthur Andersen was a bigger concern than Enron.

In the summer of 2000, Arthur Andersen officially split with its consulting arm, Andersen Consulting, and Andersen Consulting became Accenture. With the loss of its consulting services, Andersen dropped to last place among the Big Five accounting firms. Arthur Andersen had always been a network of semi-independent local offices, and each had maintained its own support personnel, such as its own director of Human Resources, all of whom reported to the managing partner of the local office. To cut costs, Andersen undertook a major reorganization to centralize many of its support functions, consistent with how the other Big Five accounting firms were organized. The local office chain of command was eliminated, and these personnel were now required to report directly to Andersen's world headquarters.

"My colleagues, both at St. Charles and at many of the local offices, were beginning to speculate that the firm was preparing for a merger. Andersen appeared to be centralizing functions, in line with the organizational structures of other accounting firms. There were other little things going on that, by themselves, were very insignificant but when you looked at them in the aggregate, made me wonder if the firm was getting ready for a merger," Jill explained. Some people were laid off as part of the reorganization. Jill sipped her tea and looked up, "Then September 11 came along, and then Enron happened in October, and whatever deal might have been in the works fell apart."

The day after Memorial Day in May 2001, the managing partner for Andersen's training center in St. Charles held a meeting with all the staff to announce that the facility was going to centralize functions, too. "That's when things started to change," Jill said.

Repercussions from the Enron situation had not yet hit St. Charles, but things were becoming bleak. People were starting to be laid off, and courses were being eliminated to cut costs. "Every manager had to identify nonessential training, and I thought this is silly. We don't have nonessential training. Who in their right mind would make the business decision to offer nonessential training? But nevertheless, we all went through the exercise." Some staff were choosing to leave voluntarily. "They could see the writing on the wall that it was not going to be as good a place as it had been. They didn't like the changes, the central-ization, the general working conditions, or the layoffs. Those of us who were left were looking over our shoulders and saying, *Am I going to have enough work to do? Are they going to fire me, too?*"

The indictment of Andersen was announced publicly March 14, 2002. "After that, there were headlines practically every day saying another client had dropped Andersen. We speculated that the govern-ment needed someone to sacrifice because they didn't have enough information to get Enron." St. Charles staff participated in marches and protests against the indictment that were held in the Chicago area. "We were on quite the roller coaster the whole time, and then we got the rug pulled out from under us."

By the middle of April, all training had been suspended. Andersen announced that they were going to lay off 40 percent of the training staff. With the sharp drop in clients, the business wasn't there.

There were only about 300 people assigned to the St. Charles loca-tion by this time. At 8 o'clock on a Monday evening in April 2002, each staff person received a voice message. Depending on which voice message was received, each person learned either that he or she should show up for work the next day or was unemployed. The remaining employees were told that, with some hard work, the firm could weather this storm. Three days later, Andersen fired the remaining personnel at the training center. "The indictment was in March and the trial was in May. What happened in those three days in the middle of April that told the top levels of the firm we are going down?" Jill questioned.

She took her empty teacup over to the kitchen sink and continued speaking:

> I keep thinking of other cases where companies had done wrong. When the Exxon Valdez dumped oil in the ocean and destroyed the Alaskan coastline, Exxon pinned the guilt on the captain very quickly, paid their fine, cleaned up the mess, and are still in business. Or the Tylenol tampering case 20 years ago; it wasn't Tylenol's fault, nevertheless, they pulled their product off the market very quickly. They took responsibility for the situation to fix the problem. Andersen didn't step up to take responsibility for the Enron problem. Granted, Enron had caused the problem by manipulating their books and by giving Andersen a false set of facts. They didn't create the situation, but they did play a part. Andersen could have salvaged its reputation by taking some responsibility. I don't think they recognized that they were losing the public relations war. It is amazing to me how quickly everything unraveled.

Today, Jill Myers is attending the MBA program at Northwestern University in Chicago. Her former colleagues from Arthur Andersen have found jobs at other firms, including Deloitte & Touche, Sears, AllState, and PricewaterhouseCoopers. She continues to question the government's decision to prosecute the entire firm instead of the individuals who were directly involved. "I don't know the law, so I can't say the government is wrong to do what they did, but I continue to believe that Enron caused far more damage to create this situation, and I don't see that they paid quite the same price that Andersen did."

Closing Up Shop

By March 2002, entire offices outside the U.S. were leaving Andersen to join other firms. Many of the firm's partners focused on ensuring the safety of those under them. Some partners took whole groups of people with them to other firms and corporations. Other Andersen employees started new firms together. Many older partners decided to retire but continued to use their business contacts to help as many Andersen employees as possible find new employment.

At Arthur Andersen's Houston offices, there had once been 1,700 employees on 15 floors of the Pennzoil Tower, but by August 2002, only a skeleton crew was left to close up shop. Of the 28,000 U.S. firm's members, between 200 and 300 remain in two offices at this writing. Those familiar with Andersen were not surprised that the firm made strong efforts to "take care of its own" at the end. One former Andersen partner said, "You can take away my position, and you can jail my partner, but you can't prevent me from helping my people. You can take away my email, you can take away my computer, you can take away my firm, but you can't silence my voice."[11]

References

1. McRoberts, Flynn. 2002. "Repeat Offender Gets Stiff Justice." *Chicago Tribune*, September 4.

2. McRoberts, Flynn. 2002. "Repeat Offender Gets Stiff Justice." *Chicago Tribune*, September 4.

3. McRoberts, Flynn. 2002. "Repeat Offender Gets Stiff Justice." *Chicago Tribune*, September 4.

4. Gordon, M., "Labor Secretary to Address Enron Hearings," Associated Press (online), February 6, 2002.

5. McRoberts, Flynn. 2002. "Repeat Offender Gets Stiff Justice," *Chicago Tribune*, September 4.

6. McRoberts, Flynn. 2002. "Repeat Offender Gets Stiff Justice," *Chicago Tribune*, September 4.

7. McRoberts, Flynn. 2002. "Repeat Offender Gets Stiff Justice," *Chicago Tribune*, September 4.

8. Individuals in this and other stories are real people. Their names have been changed or omitted to provide confidentiality.

9. Individuals in this and other stories are real people. Their names have been changed or omitted to provide confidentiality.

10. Individuals in this and other stories are real people. Their names have been changed or omitted to provide confidentiality.

11. Partner interview.

WILL ANYTHING
REALLY CHANGE?

Regulating the Accounting Industry

In March 2003, Brendon McDonald, a former Arthur Andersen auditor, was arrested on charges that, in September 2001—a month before David Duncan began shredding at Enron—he had deleted emails, shredded documents, and otherwise helped American Tissue, a paper company, destroy records related to accusations of accounting fraud.[1] In March 2003, Bristol-Myers Squibb lowered revenue by $2.5 billion in a restatement of financials between 1999 and 2001, citing errors and inappropriate accounting.[2] About the same time, WorldCom announced that it had to write-down $79.8 billion in assets and goodwill.[3] The story of trouble in U.S. business continues to unfold.

Large public accounting firms, such as Arthur Andersen, lost their way in the 1990s. As Arthur Levitt has put it, the American economic system became a web of dysfunctional relationships, with a lot of good people getting caught in a bad system[4]—a system so full of loopholes and gaps that it was a free-for-all for dishonest people or those easily corrupted or co-opted. Arthur Andersen's story is not just a story about shifting values and unexpected consequences within the firm, it is also a case for reform in the public accounting system—reform that addresses the fundamental conflict between serving the public interest and making money. Such reform would significantly change the business of public accounting in the U.S.

There was an initial flurry of activity in the wake of the Enron scandal, and both the U.S. Senate and the House of Representatives launched investigations. Most of these actions focused on catching and punishing those involved in financial wrongdoing. Hoping to constrain corporate executives and encourage auditors to do the right thing,[5] new sets of regulations were also enacted and additional funding was provided to monitor and prosecute those who break the new rules.

Securities and Exchange Commission

In July 2002, President George W. Bush publicly announced a significant increase in the SEC's budget, from $438 million allocated in 2002 to $776 million—a 77 percent increase. In late February 2003, William H. Donaldson became the new head of the SEC. In his first appearance before Congress on March 13, 2003, he testified that it would take time to improve the SEC's oversight. With a budget increase, his plan is to review and reorganize the agency's operations, upgrade the agency's now-antiquated computer systems, and hire 800 lawyers, accountants, investigators, and other employees, bringing the SEC's staff up to 4,000.

The agency never received the large budget increase it was promised. Less than three months after announcing the $776 million budget, the administration said it supported an appropriation of $568 million.[6] Congress overrode this reduction in the increase and the Senate passed a measure authorizing $656 million for 2003. As of February 2003, the SEC 2003 budget was technically not settled by Congress.

Highlights of the Sarbanes-Oxley Corporate Reform Act of 2002

In 2002, President George W. Bush also signed into law a sweeping effort at corporate governance and accounting industry reforms, the Sarbanes-Oxley Corporate Reform Act. The Act applies to publicly held companies and their audit firms, as well as to CPAs, whether they work as external auditors or are employed by a publicly traded company. The Act requires all CEOs and CFOs of U.S.-registered companies to provide a statement to accompany the auditor's report that personally certifies the honesty of the financial reports.

In the wake of the Enron scandal, the first certifications were requested of the 200 largest U.S.-registered companies. But these requirements applied only to U.S.-registered companies—those companies registered offshore were not compelled to make these certifications. Many of the companies that recently failed, including WorldCom and Global Crossing, Ltd., were registered offshore. Accenture Ltd., the public company formed when Andersen Consulting dissolved the partnership with Arthur Andersen, is registered in Bermuda but complied voluntarily.

If the CEO or CFO files financials that are not in compliance with reporting requirements, he or she must reimburse the company for any bonus or equity-based compensation received during the year following a noncompliant document, along with any profits realized from the sale of stock during that period. Maximum penalties for willing and knowing violations related to CEO or CFO certifications are $5 million in fines and/or up to 20 years in prison. "Willing and knowing" is what makes it difficult to convict on this and other charges. The burden of proof to demonstrate intent is on the government and is made difficult to meet. In the first test of this law, in March 2003, criminal charges were brought against the CEO and CFO of HealthSouth, a health care company, for reporting more than $1 billion in nonexistent profits.[7]

To remove the perceived conflict of interest between accounting and consulting, the Act made it unlawful for a firm to provide nonaudit services, including tax services, unless the activities are preapproved by the client company board's audit committee. The preapproval requirement is waived if the nonaudit services are less than 5 percent of the total fees paid for the audit. The Act also banned eight categories of nonaudit services. These are:

1. Bookkeeping or other services related to the accounting records or financial statements of an audit client

2. Financial information systems design and implementation

3. Appraisal or valuation services, fairness opinions, or contribution-in-kind reports

4. Actuarial services

5. Internal audit outsourcing services

6. Management functions or human resources selection functions

7. Broker or dealer investment advising or investment banking services

8. Legal services and expert services unrelated to the audit

In February 2003, the Enron investigation uncovered evidence of massive tax evasion that implicated both Arthur Andersen and Deloitte & Touche. Deloitte had audited some of Enron's SPEs. If people thought the SPE schemes were elaborate beyond understanding, the fact that it took a year and a half to find the trail of tax evasion is pause for thought.

When the Act was being written, some lawmakers also wanted to put strict bans on tax services, but accounting industry lobbyists fought hard to keep this lucrative business and opposed further curbs on tax consulting.[8] Accounting firms succeeded in getting the SEC to back down on forbidding auditors to provide tax-planning services.[9] Critics saw this defeat as an alarming sign that the effort to reform had begun to slide backward.

Auditor rotation was another significant issue that many felt needed to be addressed. Although the Sarbanes-Oxley Act does not require corporations to change accounting firms, it does require a rotation of lead audit partners and any reviewing partner from a client account after five years; they can return after five years. It also requires junior partners to rotate out after seven years; they can return after two years. The General Accounting Office (GAO) of the federal government was directed to study the potential affects of stronger measures that would require mandatory rotation of the entire audit firm. This is important. In the Enron case, Andersen had been its auditor for over 16 years—a period during which it had sold Enron consulting and internal audit outsourcing services, and Andersen expected its annual fees to reach $100 million in 2002. If audit firms know they have a limited number of years with the client, they may be less likely to bend to client pressures.

In reaction to another Enron practice known as "the revolving door" (Enron's hiring of former Andersen auditors), the Act prohibits a firm from providing audit services if any of the company's top officials, such as the CEO or CFO, were employed by the audit firm during the one-year period before the audit. A longer period of three to five years was suggested but rejected.

Document retention is specifically addressed in the Act, requiring auditors to retain their work papers on audits for five years. Penalties for tampering with records, destroying documents, or otherwise impeding an investigation can be up to 20 years' imprisonment and may include fines. The statute of limitations for securities fraud was set at five years from the fraud, and penalties and fines were increased, allowing up to 10 years' imprisonment. Penalties for wire and mail fraud were increased from five to ten years of imprisonment. Many believe the statute of limitations should extend beyond five years.

At Enron, executives had withheld information from Andersen and the board's audit committee, and misrepresented information to the committee by telling it that Andersen auditors had approved practices when they hadn't. New rules that had been issued under Levitt's term with the SEC relating to the independence of audit committees and the relationship of auditors to the committee were incorporated into the Act. The Act requires that the composition of the audit committee must include one individual with extensive financial knowledge, and the Act attempts to make the communication between auditors and audit committees more direct and independent of company executives.

Whistle-blowers are also protected and allowed to collect attorney fees and special damages that arise from their role in bringing wrongdoing to light. Some protections were already in place. The first thing Ken Lay, CEO of Enron, did after Sherron Watkins met with him about her concerns was to contact his legal people to see whether he could fire her. The lawyer's response was that he could, under Texas law, but the lawyer advised against it because that risked her going public right away with her findings.

Personal loans by companies to executives are now prohibited by the Act. Along with accounting tricks, it was revealed that companies were loaning executives large sums and allowing them to use their stock options or stock as collateral, so that when the stock became worthless, companies were left holding the bag.

Public Company Accounting Oversight Board

The centerpiece of the Act is the creation of the Public Company Accounting Oversight Board, which replaces the accounting industry's self-regulatory Public Oversight Board and merges functions and powers of other groups into one entity with broad oversight responsibilities. The new board has authority to set and adopt standards in areas including: auditing and related financial statement certification, quality control, ethics, independence, and "other standards necessary to protect the public interest."[10] The SEC retains oversight and enforcement authority over the new board, including the power to censure the board or impose limitations on its activities, functions, and operations, as well as the power to approve, amend, or reject the board's proposed rules.

The Act established board membership of five, two of which must be or must have been CPAs. The other three must not be or have been CPAs. Many believed the board was too small and called for at least nine members, with two or three being CPAs but not having a vote on disciplinary matters that come before the board.[11]

The Public Company Accounting Oversight Board has responsibility for registering public accounting firms. Previously, firms registered directly with the SEC.

Importantly, the board is charged with conducting inspections of accounting firms' audits. Previously, the oversight system relied on investigations opened by the SEC as a reactive measure to evidence of wrongdoing. The board is empowered to initiate investigations of potential violations of securities laws, accounting and financial reporting standards, and the competence and conduct of auditors.

The board can conduct disciplinary proceedings and impose sanctions. Final sanctions imposed by the board must be reported to the SEC, which has the power to enhance, modify, cancel, reduce, or require remission of a sanction. Disciplinary hearings are to be closed unless the board orders them to be public, for cause, and with consent of the parties. The public will not get a report of sanctions until the party being sanctioned exhausts the appeal process.

Critics of the Sarbanes-Oxley Act believe disciplinary hearings should be more public because the investigation and appeals process can potentially take years. It is difficult to balance protecting the rights of CPAs under review with the public's right to know whether auditors are being investigated.

The mechanisms for funding the board have also been criticized. The Public Company Accounting Oversight Board is funded through assessments on accounting firms and their corporate clients. This raises concerns about whether the investigations of the board will be extensive and vigorous enough to protect the public interest. The board's financial dependence on those it is supposed to oversee went against recommendations for real reform that would ensure independence of the board.

Finally, those in favor of strong reform believe the ability of audit clients to "go opinion shopping" and engage in competitive bidding gives clients too much power over audit firms. To reduce the conflict that accounting firms face between working for the public and getting and keeping clients, many would like to see the board or SEC take the responsibility for hiring auditors and collecting audit fees.

New Financial Accounting Standards Board (FASB) Rules

It does matter who makes the rules, and it is difficult to expect the accounting industry to set its own rules, given the conflicts of interest built into a public accounting system where auditors are hired by those they audit. The FASB is funded by fees assessed to public corporations, and when it caved to pressures on the issue of expensing stock options, this was seen by many as evidence that it was a failed institution. The Public Company Accounting Oversight Board did not replace the FASB, a private-sector panel, and it still has accounting rule-making functions. However, rule making was restructured under the Sarbanes-Oxley Act to offset the negative effects of auditors advocating for clients, giving the new Public Company Accounting Oversight Board an important role.

On March 13, 2003, the FASB announced that it would overhaul rules for expensing stock options within the next 12 months,[12] buying more time for an issue on which the FASB had already spent years. Stock options are now widely used for all ranks of employees, and an annual executive pay survey found that the CEOs of 23 large companies under investigation for alleged malfeasance earned an average of $62 million in stock options in 2001, compared with an average of $36 million for all CEOs in 1999.[13] Whether the FASB will require stock options to be expensed in the financial statements or buried in footnotes in the statement remains to be seen—if more disclosure is, in fact, even required.

The issue of stock options is also a concern of the SEC. In his testimony before Congress, William Donaldson, head of the SEC, indicated a belief that companies need to account for stock options granted executives but questioned whether recording them as expenses was the most accurate way to reflect their cost.[14] However, Donaldson also said that he would wait for the rules proposed by the FASB before taking any action. Many, including Warren Buffet, Arthur Levitt, and some former partners at Arthur Andersen, may have been disappointed by this position. They believe the stock option issue is one of the most central problems in the system and that any equivocation on how options are expensed will leave a critical issue unresolved. However, whatever decision the FASB makes, the new Public Company Oversight Board has the authority to amend, modify, repeal, and reject any standards suggested by groups such as the FASB. The SEC then has the oversight power to amend, modify, repeal, or reject any standards set by the new oversight board.

Although there are limits to how much the SEC can do about what executives are paid, it can require disclosure and take steps to address the dilution of stock values created by issuing too many stock options to employees. If steps are not taken to address the issue of executive compensation, the culture of business that led to failure cannot be expected to change.

The FASB also took action to strengthen disclosure of off-balance-sheet transactions, such as the SPEs at Enron. In February 2002, the FASB made a new rule requiring that outsiders had to put up 10% of an SPE's capital and that capital must be at risk for it to qualify to be off the books. Ironically, Arthur Andersen had proposed the 10% rule several years ago. In another case of what some believe is backsliding, in June 2002, the FASB changed the rule again so that it might theoretically be more than 10% or less than the original 3%. "Now the 10% number is fixed in sand as a 'rebuttable presumption.' Companies and their auditors will decide what level is reasonable, based on a bunch of criteria."[16] Said Lynn Turner, former Chief Account for the SEC, "They will use it to beat the auditors down. The auditors will never tell them no."[17]

Both SPEs and derivatives remain largely unregulated. There is also the question of allowing the practice of one company paying another company to put an SPE on its books. Derivatives are contracts for futures, swaps, and forward options; at Enron, these were known as "virtual assets." Enron had shifted from being a hard-asset-based company, owning pipelines and energy for sale, to being more or less an investment bank engaged in trading in "virtual assets." This is where Enron met its downfall. The mark-to-market valuation of these contracts was an unusual practice, and it was questionable whether it was technically legal, but everyone let it slide, convinced by Enron's arguments that this was a New Economy model and that the old rules were wrong for today's business. Enron booked the total value of multi-year contracts using mark-to-market at the end of each month. Some people believe this is what created the short-term mentality at Enron. Rather than taking the value of contracts in increments of months or years, each month, the slate was wiped clean, which drove a frenzied sales dynamic.

A similar situation to Enron occurred with Long-Term Capital Management, a hedge fund based on unregulated derivatives, which collapsed in 1998. Because this threatened the global economy, the government bailed out the fund at a cost of $4.6 billion.

Statements are being made that the regulation of derivatives will be looked into, but some find it discouraging that regulation for derivatives has been "looked into" for more than two decades with almost no results. Other people, such as Warren Buffet, believe the complex structures of derivatives are a ticking time bomb in the economy, and if it explodes, recent events will pale in comparison.

Establishing the Public Company Accounting Oversight Board

Once Sarbanes-Oxley was enacted, it was crucial to select a person with impeccable credentials to chair the board if it was to have credibility. Harvey Pitt, head of the SEC, made a choice that proved to be his downfall. Because Pitt had represented accounting firms in many matters against the SEC prior to becoming the head of the SEC, he came under heavy criticism for seeming lenient with accounting firms and too aligned with corporate interests. Pitt's record created doubts about his ability to lead reform.

Pitt appointed William H. Webster to head the new Public Company Accounting Oversight Board. Webster accepted the appointment, then immediately resigned when conflicts of interest involving his past dealings as chairman of the audit committee of U.S. Technologies were revealed. This was the last straw for Pitt, and he resigned his position at the SEC in November 2002. But he remained as a lame-duck chairman for months until William H. Donaldson, former chair of the New York Stock Exchange, was approved and replaced him in February 2003.

"Never has there been a slower start"[18] to establishing an entity enacted by legislation. At the end of 2002, the board had no chairman, did not have a full board, did not have a budget or funding, had no staff, no office, and no plan. Lacking a permanent chair, the board held its first meeting on January 10, 2003, with Charles D. Niemeier presiding as acting chair. The actions taken at the first meeting included the following:

- The board's first decision was to reject a symbolic proposal made by Kayla J. Gillan, a board member, to rotate the board's own auditors every five years to assure their independence.

- The board members voted themselves annual salaries of $452,000 per year, with the chair, once selected, to receive $560,000 per year. It is also offering some of the best salaries for public service jobs in Washington for other positions: The general counsel will receive $425,000; the director of external communications, $250,000; the deputy director in charge of registration, $300,000.

- A decision to retain Korn/Ferry International, an executive search firm, to find people to fill the top seven staff jobs was ratified. Korn/Ferry will receive $60,000 for each position it fills.

- A request to borrow $1.9 million from the government to meet its expenses for the first month was ratified.

- The board ratified its lease for its Washington offices, space that was vacated by Arthur Andersen after it collapsed.

Overall, there is concern that the Public Company Oversight Board is not a great improvement over the now-defunct Public Oversight Board. The board is funded through assessments on accounting firms and their corporate clients. Many believe that this can compromise its independence. If not funded at a level that will make the inspection process meaningful, it could become a sham.[19]

On April 15, 2003, the SEC announced its selection of William J. McDonough, the longtime president of the Federal Reserve Bank of New York, to be chairman of the Public Company Accounting Board.

Backsliding

With new scandals surfacing daily, the story is still unfolding, and the question of whether real reform will happen continues to be relevant. But the accounting industry has a powerful lobbying presence in Washington, and these lobbying groups put pressure on Congressional representatives to water down legislation almost before the ink was dry, raising the question of whether any meaningful reform could happen at all.

At the time that the media raised public awareness of Enron's failure, Congress and the Bush administration were embarrassed by revelations that significant campaign contributions had been paid by Enron and the accounting industry. Such large campaign contributions continue to be donated and lobbying firms are paid to support the interests of the accounting industry and corporate clients. Such pressures and payments concern critics who point to the experiences Arthur Levitt documented in his book, *Take on the Street*.[20] During his efforts to institute reform while head of the SEC, Levitt told of receiving letters from congressmen who threatened to cut the SEC's budget if he did not back away from his reform efforts.

Although some politicians who had received Enron contributions returned them to be distributed to employees of Enron, there is no reason to believe that politicians will not continue to accept contributions from the accounting industry. It is the opinion of many reform-minded people that public accounting firms should not be allowed to make campaign contributions or employ lobbyists because of their special role as a quasi-governmental industry, charged with protecting the public interest and the U.S. financial markets. Nor should politicians accept donations from an industry they are charged with directly overseeing. Such resources could be better spent in improving accounting methods and preventing fraud and abuse.

There was considerable backsliding and "as the public [became] distracted by the threatened war with Iraq, they [Congress] began backsliding in earnest," and "Michael Oxley [co-author of the Sarbanes-Oxley Act, led] the retreat."[21] As the Enron scandal has receded from people's minds and Arthur Andersen becomes a footnote in public accounting's history, will Congress take up the challenge of true systemwide reform in business, the accounting industry, and the U.S. government? The "democratization" of the stock market may, however, have an unexpected effect. The millions of individuals who lost their savings and pensions in the recent failures are likely to have long memories.

References

1. Deutsch, Claudia, H. 2003. "Accountant and Paper Company Chief Face Fraud Charges," *The New York Times*, March 11, p. C4.

2. Abelson, Reed. 2003. "Bristol-Myers Lowers Revenue by $2.5 Billion in Restatement," *The New York Times*, March 11, p. C1.

3. Romero, Simon. 2003. "WorldCom Decides to Take $79 Billion Write-Down," *The New York Times*, March 14, p. C2.

4. Levitt, Arthur Jr. 2002. *Take on the Street*, New York: Pantheon.

5. Byrnes, Nanette et al. 2002. "The Enron Scandal: Accounting in Crisis," *Business Week Online*, January 28.

6. Labaton, Stephen. 2003. "Six Months Later, New Audit Board Holds First Talk," *The New York Times*, January 10, p. A1.

7. Norris, Floyd, 2003. "Hospital Chain Accused of Huge Accounting Fraud," *The New York Times*, March 20, pp. C1 and C4.

8. Schroeder, Michael. 2002. "Accounting Industry Is Taken to Task," *The Wall Street Journal*, March 8, p. A12.

9. "Downsized Corporate Reforms," *The New York Times*, January 23, 2003, p. A24.

10. American Institute of Certified Public Accountants. 2003. "How the Sarbanes-Oxley Act of 2002 Impacts the Accounting Profession," *aicpa.org/info/Sarbanes-Oxley2002.asp*, Accessed March 14, 2003.

11. Frontline, *Bigger Than Enron*, PBS Video, 2002.

12. "Accounting Panel to Overhaul Regulations on Stock Options," *The New York Times*, March 13, 2003, p. C5.

13. United for a Fair Economy & Institute for Policy Studies, "CEOs Who Cooked the Books Earned 70% More," *Business Week*, September 2002.

14. Labaton, Stephen. 2003. "S.E.C. Chief Says Fixing the Agency Will Take Time," *The New York Times*, March 14, p. C5.

15. Norris, Floyd. 2002. "Accounting Reform: A Bright Line Vanishes," *The New York Times*, June 7, p. C1.

16. Norris, Floyd 2002. "Accounting Reform: A Bright Line Vanishes," *The New York Times*, June 7, p. C1.

17. Norris, Floyd. 2002. "Accounting Reform: A Bright Line Vanishes," *The New York Times*, June 7, p. C1.

18. Norris, Floyd. 2002. "Will Auditing Reform Die before It Begins?" *The New York Times*, December 27, p. C1.

19. Norris, Floyd. 2002. "Help Wanted at the S.E.C.; Help Needed for Reforms," *The New York Times*, November 13, p. C1.

20. Levitt, Arthur. 2002. *Take on the Street*, New York: Pantheon, p. 118.

21. Krugman, Paul. 2002. "Fool Me Once," *The New York Times*, October 8, p. A1.

10

CONCLUSIONS: ANDERSEN AND CONFLICTS IN THE PUBLIC ACCOUNTING SYSTEM

Andersen's shift from a public accounting firm to a multiservice organization took many twists and unexpected turns during its 90-year rise and eventual fall. During this time, Andersen found itself in an increasingly competitive and deregulated business environment, and the firm responded by making decisions that allowed it to adapt to these changing business conditions. You can look back over time and see how each decision—and the external forces shaping those decisions—moved the firm steadily away from its core business and values.

The accumulated consequences of the external pressures and internal decisions played out in the 1990s, during a time of high expectation for New Economy investing and financial speculation for short-term profit. The firm's final adaptation to this external business environment—and the one that proved fatal—was Arthur Andersen's 1992 decision to shift to a sales culture that rewarded partners for bringing in and keeping clients. The decision was explained as a move to boost

163

profit, but it was symbolic of much deeper and conflicting issues. Introducing such a strong sales culture created a conflict of interest between the firm's growth and profitability and its protection of the public trust. Empowered to make their own decisions, some local office partners drifted into situations where that conflict of interest compromised Andersen's core values and clouded partner judgment.

As Andersen's clients became risk takers, so did the firm. After 1992, Arthur Andersen found itself in a series of serious litigations, including Arizona Baptist Foundation, Sunbeam Corporation, and Waste Management. Although Andersen did not admit or deny wrongdoing in these cases, they were symptomatic of the higher risk environment. The consequences of taking such risks all finally came together at Enron.

It was not simply greed that brought Arthur Andersen down, as some would like you to believe, although greed did play its part. Andersen's partners found themselves caught up in the corporate greed of the 1990s, and they pushed for a piece of the action. Although partner compensation jumped from an average of around $130,000 in the early 1980s to $450,000 by 2000, this was nothing compared with the high salaries and lucrative stock options being given to executives in big corporations during the same time period. At Enron, for example, 28 executives and board members made $1,190,479,472 between October 1998 and November 2001 by exercising their stock options.[1]

Nor did Andersen's collapse come entirely as the result of conflicting interests between consulting and auditing, although that played a part, as well. Before Arthur Andersen and Andersen Consulting split, the firm had grown into a global multiservice firm, bringing in over $16 billion in annual revenue. More than half the growth and profits were from consulting. Andersen's consultants certainly gave the auditors a taste for success. But Arthur Andersen had always had a successful consulting service, and for most of its 90 years, consulting and audit had worked side by side seemingly without any serious compromises of the firm's values and audit standards.

In the end, Arthur Andersen's story is about the conflicted environment in which public accounting operates in the U.S.—a conflict between serving the public and maintaining profitability. Although Andersen's partners must carry some of the blame for the firm's fall, they were also caught in a system where manipulating accounting guidelines and rules to please the client was often not only legal but rewarded by clients.

Although Arthur Andersen no longer conducts audits, the conflicts that Andersen faced are the conflicts that the big public accounting firms still face. It is this industry-wide cultural system, that is the real culprit behind Andersen's fall. Other accounting firms also teeter on the same brink over which Andersen stumbled. The fall of Andersen is a tale of incremental change, punctuated by a small number of major shifts in values that had unexpected consequences, and understanding the system that prompted these shifts is essential for implementing effective reform.

The First Twists—Partner Independence

Andersen was founded during a time when ethical considerations of social responsibility and stewardship were clear. Arthur E. Andersen, the firm's founder, wrote and spoke often about the role of accounting in protecting the public interest and the auditor's responsibility to know the "facts behind the figures" and to "stand up to management" *for* the investor. For Andersen and his accountants, their role as stewards of the public trust seemed straightforward, and Andersen folklore was full of stories about how Arthur E. Andersen walked away from important clients who asked him to violate his principles and the public trust. This period is idealized as a golden age of accounting, and many would like to see public accounting firms return to the standards and principles of that time.

In the wake of Arthur Andersen's fall, there have been calls to reestablish credibility in the accounting industry. "Let's get back to basics," *Business Week* has pleaded.[2] The AICPA's new chairman of the board, William F. Ezzell, agrees and wants to reestablish the image of professional accounting as a *"profession*, not a trade"[3] and return to its core purpose of protecting the public interest. In his first statement to the AICPA's 350,000 members, Ezzell said accountants have obligations beyond rules and regulations to do "what *we* believe *we* must do to protect the public interest,"[4] and urged CPAs "to live by their core values."[5] His list of core values is very like Arthur E. Andersen's early principles:

- An unwavering commitment to a code of ethics
- A distinct and evolving body of knowledge
- A sense of duty to the public interest
- Standards of excellence
- A shared sense of purpose

Calling for a renewal of values is a fine ideal, but expecting accountants to return to past values without any other changes in the accounting industry is overly optimistic. The accounting industry operating today is a very different industry than it was when, for example, Arthur Andersen & Co. was founded. None of the original accounting firms were designed for today's bigger and more complex businesses.

During his time, Arthur E. Andersen could not have anticipated the changes from strict auditing based on accounting principles to increasingly sophisticated and computerized accounting based on guideline interpretation. Standing up for accounting principles and walking away from a client did not carry the same kind of financial consequence that walking away from a multimillion-dollar engagement does today. Although, in more than one case, Arthur E. Andersen put the viability of his firm at risk and greatly diminished partner earnings, the firm was small, audit was a thriving service, and the stakes were not quite so high.

His legacies of integrity and honesty, the One-Firm, One-Voice Partnership Model, and training to a shared method established the firm's reputation but, as business changed, the firm had to adapt to survive.

After Arthur E. Andersen's death, one of the first changes to the partnership agreement made the partners equal as equity holders in the firm with a "one-partner, one-vote" policy. This decision to democratize Arthur Andersen & Co. shifted the center of power—increasing the independence granted to local offices while decreasing centralized control. This democratic governance system permitted local office partners to make their own decisions, build their own local business, and in some cases, to overrule an opinion from headquarters. Granting the local offices more independence was a trade-off that allowed Arthur Andersen to adapt to the new global economy and to grow.

Another Turn—The Effects of Growth

Growth at Arthur Andersen was initially driven by the post-World War II global expansion of corporations and was possible, in part, because of Andersen's ability to offer a combination of audit and consulting services. With local office's independence, the firm had the flexibility to respond quickly and effectively to business conditions around the world. But size has its limits, and the firm's partnership structure was not designed to manage an organization of Andersen's increasing size. It was only a matter of time before Andersen would grow so big that the firm would have to make modifications in its organization to manage its larger size and geographic spread. Growth fragmented the firm by geographic distance—and by service line—when Andersen reorganized into divisions. Division into smaller units solved some span-of-control issues but diluted communication, divided the one voice of the partnership, and shifted partner allegiances from the partnership to the division level, where informal exchange systems were encouraged to build the business.

With size, there also came complexity. Geographic divisions, business divisions, practice divisions, and industry divisions added increasingly complex layers. By the end of the 1990s, the firm structurally had become more like a giant multinational corporation than a partnership, although partners retained a measure of control over their own local offices.

Growth and complexity also created the conditions for rogue partners to emerge. The size of the partnership had gone far beyond the ability of its members to maintain personal relationships and personal trust. Andersen's response to growth unexpectedly divided the firm more deeply than intended and was responsible for loss of central control, giving even more power to the local offices and eventually allowing David Duncan to make decisions about Enron's audit that ignored the advice of Andersen's Professional Standards Group.

Impact of Consulting Services

Arthur E. Andersen had left his firm with another legacy—consulting. Despite advice from other accountants, he believed that consulting could be contained and integrity would be maintained by the accounting profession's strong standards and principles. As long as consulting remained a small part of Arthur Andersen's overall business, it was indeed contained.

But the lifting of the bans on solicitation and advertising in the accounting industry during the 1970s, along with flattening revenue growth from audit, put Andersen at a turning point. The partners responded to these external business pressures in 1979 by giving the green light to expand Andersen's consulting. It now seems a questionable decision, given the attention the SEC was paying to consulting services within public accounting firms. But the partners felt that it was a necessary move to keep the firm financially stable as revenue growth from audit services decreased, competition increased, and litigations grew.

From the start, there were consequences. The cultures of account-ing and consulting were quite distinct and never really compatible. Auditing is about stability. Consulting is about change. Whereas accountants follow and implement rules, consultants evaluate and change rules. This difference made consultants an uncertain, even risky element in the firm's strictly controlled workforce. The differences ulti-mately resulted in such deep conflicts that the two services ended up in arbitration by 1997.

But in 1979, profits could be made in consulting, and this would stabilize the firm during a rocky time. As the firm adapted to the exter-nal business environment by growing consulting, partners had no way of knowing that conflict between accounting and consulting services would dramatically undermine Arthur Andersen's culture and core accounting profession values. Important for Andersen's story, consult-ing introduced Andersen's auditors to a more aggressive, sales-cen-tered business model. The accountants experienced the rewards that a successful consulting service could deliver. Both made a deep impres-sion, and the firm's culture was influenced by the profits that a suc-cessful consulting practice could bring in. Although it was not intended, the new model encouraged client service and sales over stewardship and protecting the public interest.

Andersen Adopts a Sales Culture

Andersen's accounting partners may not have been so ready to adopt the more aggressive sales culture modeled by consulting if Andersen Consulting had not split off from accounting as a separate business unit in 1988. This split removed a significant portion of Arthur Andersen's revenue base and pushed the partnership to the 1992 partner purge. The purge revealed how very far Arthur Andersen had drifted from its tradi-tional values and marked a shift in dominance from the more tradi-tional partners to new, auditor-salesman partners. At the same time, compensation was changed to motivate selling, performance evaluation emphasized sales ability, training included salesmanship, and aggressive sales targets were established.

In an unprecedented event, the 1992 partner purge removed 10 percent of Arthur Andersen's partners. The Andersen leaders driving the purge thought they were adapting to the more competitive business environment and that they were doing the right thing for the firm. The partner purge displaced the more conservative partners who held traditional Andersen values with younger, more performance-oriented partners; it made public a number of value and behavioral shifts that prioritized the sales role for Arthur Andersen partners and undercut the values on which Andersen's early reputation and success had been based.

After the purge, Andersen had clearly adopted a more client-friendly approach to accounting than it had favored in the past, and generating work through sales became an increasingly important performance measure. Accounting partners intensified efforts to build sales networks, modeling their activities on those of consulting.

But this does not mean that Andersen's core values, especially integrity, were abandoned by everyone. Barbara Toffler, who has written about ethics at Arthur Andersen, admits she found no "smoking gun" during the time she worked at the firm in the late 1990s.[6] However, partners, most of whom had never worked anywhere else, were under enormous pressure to meet sales targets or face possible dismissal. These pressures certainly clouded judgment for some.

Although many local offices remained quite conservative, some partners clearly compromised their obligation to protect the public interest, and more placed emphasis on managing client relationships. The promotion of Andersen's services drew the firm into the high-stakes–high-rewards sales game.

After the partner purge, Arthur Andersen also found itself being watched more closely by the SEC as the firm became involved in a growing number of litigations. The threat of litigation put Arthur Andersen at risk. But Arthur Andersen either did not fully appreciate the level of that risk or was distracted by arbitration over the divorce of Arthur Andersen and Andersen Consulting. Rather than simply eliminate clients and lose revenue, Andersen tried to manage the risk.

Whether because of a failure in Andersen's risk management or an increasing partner conflict of interest between sales and stewardship, Arthur Andersen found itself in litigation one too many times. The Justice Department decided to make an example of Arthur Andersen over its audit at Enron by focusing on the obstruction of justice charge. In a press conference about the Andersen indictment, the deputy attorney general remarked that it was the intent of the Department of Justice to use Andersen's trial to send a strong message to the accounting industry that it should get its priorities straight.

The fall of Arthur Andersen is not a story about just one public accounting firm. At its root, the Andersen story is about an entire system. It is about a web of American business, government, and accounting industry problems that continue to threaten the public trust.

In the contemporary business environment of the 1990s, where corporate success was based on short-term performance, stock options, and Wall Street valuations, Arthur Andersen was not the only public accounting firm to go through this sales transformation. Throughout the accounting industry, firms began to match corporate accounting needs to appropriate accounting methods, rather than to rely on strict application of rules, much less the spirit of the rules.

Culture Change

During the latter part of the 20th century, business values changed in the U.S. as industries were privatized, deregulated and consolidated, and as organizations merged,[7] globalized, downsized, and outsourced. Along with everyone else, Andersen was pressured to change and adapt to the new economic realities. The media characterized business practices of the 1990s as a "culture of greed" and blamed Enron's "cowboy culture" for what happened there. Culture has been blamed for Andersen's fall, as well.[8] But what does it mean to blame culture?

The term *culture* has been used loosely to suggest that greed or cowboy values were widespread and acceptable. Its use obscures more than it explains. Culture does not justify individual wrongdoing, and the term provides us with little explanation about what really happened. For most people, the term *values* is more easily understood, and this is how Andersen chose to view the concept of culture.

For most people, including Andersen's partners, values are at the core of culture, and the deterioration "in the values of an industry that once prided itself on serving the public good"[9] caused the Andersen value system to degrade. Others, such as Paul Volcker, believe accounting's association with consulting led to Andersen's failure, stating, "The culture of the company changed because it got deeply involved in the consulting business."[10] Still others, including Arthur Levitt, former head of the SEC, point to changing practices from "disclosure" to one "embracing a fortress mentality."[11]

They are all right. As you have followed Andersen's journey from its early days to its final fall, you have learned how Andersen's system of values and practices changed and adapted to its internal association with consulting and to external competitive pressures. Not all of the changes were bad. Over the decades, Andersen's culture changed and adapted to survive and prosper in increasingly difficult internal and external environments. The shifts that occurred were often small, almost imperceptible, like the gradual loss of cohesiveness within the Andersen partnership. Other changes, such as the sales pressures and the 1992 partner purge, signaled major departures from Andersen's traditional values and practices.

Bringing the accounting industry back into line with the values of stewardship and the public trust will require deep, systemic changes. Putting more rules in place will help, but will not solve the underlying problems that face the accounting industry. Rules cannot fully replace personal integrity or remove the inherent conflict between serving the public and maintaining profitability. Yet many of the new reforms have succeeded only in creating more monitoring or increased fines, in the hope that these restraints will prevent corporate executives from bending the rules. Changing the values of business and the accounting profession will require change that addresses the competition among accounting firms to get and keep audit clients at any cost. To date, no one has come up with an ideal plan to reform the accounting industry. It is an enormous undertaking.

Wake-Up Call

Was Arthur Andersen's fall worth it? Long after Arthur Andersen's conviction, the question of whether it was right to indict the whole firm, rather than just those involved at Enron, is still relevant.[12] As part of its plea-bargaining with the Justice Department, the firm had presented a plan developed by Paul Volcker, an outspoken critic of the auditing firms, to reform Andersen and make it a model for the industry. Some believe this was a missed opportunity.

Eliminating Andersen has already had some unexpected negative repercussions. With Andersen's departure as an auditing firm, the number of big firms was reduced in an already dangerously consolidated industry. There are now only four big accounting firms left. All the remaining firms aggressively fought over Andersen's former clients and staff. It is ironic that, if any of the accounting firms had intentionally initiated a merger, it would have likely been denied on the basis of overconsolidating. Yet the action of the Justice Department indirectly allowed a major consolidation. Only after Andersen's fall did the federal government's GAO launch a study of the effects of consolidation within the accounting industry.

While speaking at the University of Michigan on February 4, 2003, Arthur Levitt acknowledged that the whole accounting political-economic system needs to be reformed. Rather than see Andersen fall, Levitt thinks, it would have been better to preserve the firm as a way to pressure the public accounting industry to make constructive change.[13]

To date, reforms have targeted some of the most obvious conflicts of interest in the system. But Andersen's demise has taken much of the pressure to reform off the accounting industry, and reformers such as Paul Volcker question whether reform has stalled, pointing out, "The issue we face is how far the newfound zeal for reforms will go and whether it will persist for long as Enron, Global Crossing, Xerox, WorldCom, and other accounting scandals fade from the front pages."[14]

True reforms will have to take on the critical conflict that public accounting firms face between making a profit and protecting the public. As Lynn Turner, former Chief Accountant at the SEC, remarked, "Recent events, news stories, and the business desires of public accounting firms ... raise significant public policy issues that require serious consideration."[15]

All of the big firms are troubled, and the accounting industry is in crisis.[16] Andersen's former staff hope that Andersen's story will have some value as a wake-up call in the accounting industry and for the U.S. government. As the Enron scandal recedes from people's minds, will Congress take up the challenge of true reform? To date, the answer is unclear and not entirely encouraging.

As issues more strident grab the public interest, and any object lesson gained from Andersen's demise fades and becomes less emphatic, the accounting industry, the public, and the government seem disposed to move on to other business. It will be a shame if any lesson gained here is lost and a "business as usual" mentality asserts itself, in which case, the demise of a once great company is truly an unnecessary and unproductive waste.

References

1. Bryce, Robert. 2002. *Pipe Dreams*, New York: Public Affairs.

2. Byrnes, Nanette et al. "The Enron Scandal: Can You Trust Anybody Anymore?" *Business Week Online*, January 23.

3. Ezzell, William F. 2003. "Standing Up for What We Stand For," *aicpa.org/pubs/ jofa/feb2003/ezzell.htm*, February.

4. Ezzell, William F. 2003. "Standing Up for What We Stand For," *aicpa.org/pubs/ jofa/feb2003/ezzell.htm*, February.

5. Ezzell, William F. 2003. "Standing Up for What We Stand For," *aicpa.org/pubs/ jofa/feb2003/ezzell.htm*, February.

6. Toffler, Barbara, with Jennifer Reingold. 2003. *Final Accounting: Ambition, Greed, and the Fall of Arthur Andersen*, New York: Broadway Books.

7. Surowiecki, James. 2003. "The Culture Excuse," *The New Yorker*, January 27, p. 31.

8. Eavis, Peter. 2001. "Enron Reaps What Its Cowboy Culture Sowed," thestreet.com, November 29.

9. Byrne, John A. 2002. "Joe Berardino's Fall from Grace," *Business Week Online*, August 12.

10. Byrne, John A. 2002. "Joe Berardino's Fall from Grace," *Business Week Online*, August 12.

11. Byrnes, Nanette et al. 2002. "The Enron Scandal: Accounting in Crisis" *Business Week Online*, January 28.

12. Norris, Floyd. 2002. "Will Auditing Reform Die before It Begins?" *The New York Times*, December 27, p. C1.

13. Levitt, Arthur. 2002. *Take on the Street*, New York: Pantheon, p. 66.

14. Volcker, Paul A. 2002. "A Litmus Test for Accounting Reform," *The Wall Street Journal*, May 2, p. A18.

15. Turner, Lynn. 2001. Speech given. June 28.

16. Byrne, John A. 2002. "Accounting in Crisis," *BusinessWeek Online*, January 28.

INDEX

Where to find tomorrow's best business and technology ideas. TODAY.

- Ideas for defining tomorrow's competitive strategies — and executing them.
- Ideas that reflect a profound understanding of today's global business realities.
- Ideas that will help you achieve unprecedented customer and enterprise value.
- Ideas that illuminate the powerful new connections between business and technology.

ONE PUBLISHER.
Financial Times Prentice Hall.

 **FT** Prentice Hall
FINANCIAL TIMES

WORLD BUSINESS PUBLISHER

AND 3 GREAT WEB SITES:

Business-minds.com

Where the thought leaders of the business world gather to share key ideas, techniques, resources — and inspiration.

InformIt.com

Your link to today's top business and technology experts: new content, practical solutions, and the world's best online training.

ft-ph.com

Fast access to all Financial Times Prentice Hall business books currently available.

8 reasons why you should read the Financial Times for 4 weeks RISK-FREE!

To help you stay current with significant developments in the world economy ... and to assist you to make informed business decisions — the Financial Times brings you:

 Fast, meaningful overviews of international affairs ... plus daily briefings on major world news.

 Perceptive coverage of economic, business, financial and political developments with special focus on emerging markets.

 More international business news than any other publication.

 Sophisticated financial analysis and commentary on world market activity plus stock quotes from over 30 countries.

❺ Reports on international companies and a section on global investing.

❻ Specialized pages on management, marketing, advertising and technological innovations from all parts of the world.

❼ Highly valued single-topic special reports (over 200 annually) on countries, industries, investment opportunities, technology and more.

❽ The Saturday Weekend FT section — a globetrotter's guide to leisure-time activities around the world: the arts, fine dining, travel, sports and more.

The *Financial Times* delivers a world of business news.

Use the Risk-Free Trial Voucher below!

To stay ahead in today's business world you need to be well-informed on a daily basis. And not just on the national level. You need a news source that closely monitors the entire world of business, and then delivers it in a concise, quick-read format.

With the *Financial Times* you get the major stories from every region of the world. Reports found nowhere else. You get business, management, politics, economics, technology and more.

Now you can try the *Financial Times* for 4 weeks, absolutely risk free. And better yet, if you wish to continue receiving the *Financial Times* you'll get great savings off the regular subscription rate. Just use the voucher below.

http://www.phptr.com/

Prentice Hall PTR   InformIT   InformIT Online Books   Financial Times Prentice Hall   ft.com   PTG Interactive   Reuters

TOMORROW'S SOLUTIONS FOR TODAY'S PROFESSIONALS

Prentice Hall **Professional Technical Reference**

| Browse | Book Series | What's New | User Groups | Alliances | Special Sales | Contact Us |

Search | Help | Home

Quick Search

PTR Favorites

Find a Bookstore

Book Series

Special Interests

Newsletters

Press Room

International

Best Sellers

Solutions Beyond the Book

Shopping Bag

Keep Up to Date with
PH PTR Online

We strive to stay on the cutting edge of what's happening in professional computer science and engineering. Here's a bit of what you'll find when you stop by **www.phptr.com**:

What's new at PHPTR? We don't just publish books for the professional community, we're a part of it. Check out our convention schedule, keep up with your favorite authors, and get the latest reviews and press releases on topics of interest to you.

Special interest areas offering our latest books, book series, features of the month, related links, and other useful information to help you get the job done.

User Groups Prentice Hall Professional Technical Reference's User Group Program helps volunteer, not-for-profit user groups provide their members with training and information about cutting-edge technology.

Companion Websites Our Companion Websites provide valuable solutions beyond the book. Here you can download the source code, get updates and corrections, chat with other users and the author about the book, or discover links to other websites on this topic.

Need to find a bookstore? Chances are, there's a bookseller near you that carries a broad selection of PTR titles. Locate a Magnet bookstore near you at www.phptr.com.

Subscribe today! Join PHPTR's monthly email newsletter! Want to be kept up-to-date on your area of interest? Choose a targeted category on our website, and we'll keep you informed of the latest PHPTR products, author events, reviews and conferences in your interest area.

Visit our mailroom to subscribe today! **http://www.phptr.com/mail_lists**